GOLF
CROSSWORDS

AMAZON REVIEWS ARE APPRECIATED

YouTube – Designer Ink Books
Facebook – @Designerinkbooks
designerinkbooks@gmail.com

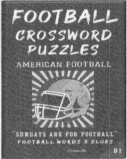

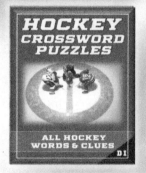

CLUE HELPERS

My Retirement Vehicle

Abbr - Abbreviation
(short) - shortened word
"word" - Focus word, AKA, or quoted
pl - plural version of clue
sl - Singular version of clue
(slang) - Less known, slang or urban
( ) important clarification e.g. year

(3wd) # of words in answer
AKA - Also Known As
NN - Nick Name
___ - Fill in the blank
No Spaces in Mult. Word answer
UPPER CASE - Acronyms
USA and **UK/CAN** English

SOLUTIONS PG 104

Find an error? Email us: Designerinkbooks@gmail.com

Across

1. Q-School finisher (short)
5. Needed after long game
9. Lose the round
14. Play "fake"
15. Bunker repair
16. Beginners clubs mass/size
17. Littered over a mini golf course
19. Hilly course is hard on it
20. The Whites, tees
21. PGA bookkeepers: Abbr
23. Illegal wedge type
24. Ladies tee box marker
25. Caddyshack's poorly received
27. Feel of weather resist shirt
30. USA C.I.C. is a 7 HDP
31. LPGA golfer Lorena O.
32. "Fantastic 4" star & 200yd driver
33. Central Coast Disc Golf
37. Mood playing hazard shot
38. Stiffest club shaft
39. Muirfield Golf Club locale
40. Hot golf market, continent
41. Being a pro golfer has few
42. Q-school, for scores
43. New clubs, fashion yearly
45. Fashionable golfer
46. Master repeat winner's Jacket reward
49. Player behind in car payments risks
50. Player's growing enemy
51. Club room rental, UK
52. Ryder Cup PGA participant
56. Golf story gets around
58. Stupid golfer
60. Best pros
61. Terrible player needs his magic
62. Targets (short)
63. Caddy advice not to go-for-it
64. Investors ___ the course to buy
65. Boston area courses

Down

1. Strange brew, course lounge
2. Believes golf stories
3. PGA Players ___ (short)
4. Downturn in gameplay
5. Golf VG, simulation'y opposite
6. Dimpled object
7. Pro can barely ___ out a win
8. "Loft" to a shot ___ arc
9. Common golfer demeanor
10. Launches golf app
11. Florida, most courses per
12. Ball hit straight as one
13. Golf marked on calendar
18. Golf course, an athletic ___
22. Cart go'er
26. Include another into 4-some
27. Lie spot after a round
28. Holes-in-one
29. Tiger's mother's heritage
30. Masters Jacket, wool & poly ___
32. Augusta, a fruitland nursery (3wd)
34. Hit ball from thick rough
35. Purposely lose a round
36. Fan going to live game
38. Caddyshack, each film segment
42. Membership contract
44. Golden Tee VG control, ___ ball
45. Most mini golf course, late 1930s
46. Ball hopped over creek
47. Course walkers are usually
48. Rewarded golfer
49. A driving type
53. Ironwood Men's Golf Assoc.
54. Tourney trims
55. Player's helper (short)
57. Consumed, from snack shack
59. After win joy

PUZZLE 1

1	2	3	4		5	6	7	8		9	10	11	12	13
14					15					16				
17			18							19				
20							21	22			23			
		24				25			26					
27	28	29				30								
31					32					33	34	35	36	
37				38					39					
40				41				42						
		43	44				45							
46	47	48				49								
50				51		52				53	54	55		
56		57		58	59									
60				61				62						
63				64				65						

Golf Fact: Original golf balls were made of wood

Across

1. Aces
5. Renaissance Golf Prod, Nasdaq
9. Different Strokes Golf Assoc.
13. Woods - power/distance level vs all clubs
14. Whippy club action
15. TOURing times players need to know: Abbr
16. International Pitch & Putt Assoc.
17. International Assoc. of Golf Travel Op.
18. Beers drank during round, for many
19. Working the flag
21. This club is as rare as Sasquatch
23. Scottish Golf Environment Group
24. Wait around for turn
25. Crypto has been paid for Fantasy prize (short)
28. Hole after the 6th
30. Shaft's rubber
32. Thomas Dickson Armour initially
33. Tournament players "bunch" in spot
37. Why your golfing son is great
39. Course Marshal keeps it like a cop
40. Pay course due
42. Caddying - show, shut and keep
45. Placing ball back in play
46. Toughen grip
48. Did Not Start, tourney status
49. Given after tourney win
51. Three Rivers Golf Assoc.
54. Heckle attempt on a swinger may what?
55. Titleist, derived from
59. Concessions
60. Caddyshack Production Co.
62. After the Masters, ___ climactic
63. CLE course water neighbor
64. "I'm never golfing AGAIN"
65. Transponder tag/chip in golf balls
66. Course lounge tacky light sign
67. European Amateur Golf Tour
68. Amount of practice needed, to score better

Down

1. Mulligan shot
2. Course open during winter?
3. Sports Network airing some golf shows
4. Craig Stadler NN
5. Hills on a driving range
6. Teammate prank
7. Small-scale lead
8. Marshal keeps the pace of play ___ like water
9. Mood when shooting well
10. Pro shop is one
11. Southern course beast (short)
12. PGA Players ___ (short)
14. Hogan's swing was said to be
20. International Golf
22. Backup golfer, or where beer is available
25. Clubhouse breakfast
26. Golf course obstacle
27. Golf crossword phrase
29. Unclear, like winter-rules
31. NN of pro is Tutta
34. Original balls, ___ wooden
35. Course needs players & a strong ___ to survive (short)
36. Practice drills, over and over
38. Rain-like, definitely not golf weather
41. Wrap hands on grip
43. Match play, out-of-turn penalty
44. Speed golf, short burst
47. Bag carrier (slang)
49. Golfer at green, pre putt
50. After round, umbrellaed drink place
52. Golf Tint (sunglass lens)
53. Cart in reverse, audio
54. Play of pro was "observed" by crowd
56. Tourney websites have all of it (short)
57. Mix(ed) reaction from Tiger gossip
58. Changes in game's flow, often (water)
61. Institute Of Golf

PUZZLE 2

1	2	3	4			5	6	7	8		9	10	11	12
13					14						15			
16					17						18			
19				20				21		22				
		23					24							
25	26	27			28		29							
30			31		32				33			34	35	36
37				38							39			
40				41			42	43	44		45			
		46			47							48		
	49	50						51		52	53			
54						55					56	57	58
59				60		61				62			
63				64					65			
66				67					68			

Golf Fact: Tiger Woods made his first hole-in-one at 8 years old

Across

1. Ball "contacts" rock
5. Iowa Golf Assoc. Found.
9. Tenn. Golf Course Super. Assoc.
14. Contract "ment"
15. Excess wrist in shot, a real ___
16. Mickelson timers
17. "Wander" the course
18. Player's growing list
19. Backswing to head
20. Some tee box markers, mixed look
22. Upper body swinging look
24. US Open low age limit
25. Cart starter (short)
26. PGA Players what? (short)
27. The course lavatory AKA
32. Membership terms are OK
34. "Angered" golfer
35. Player's health advisors: Abbr
36. Golf TV, btw shows
37. When club touches ball
41. Golf scores "weighed"
44. NN - J-Ro
46. Bonding between shots
47. Pro travel lodgings
48. Popular golf equipment
52. Bobby Jones birth town, GA
56. Rare iron, hard to hit
57. Brand name on ball
58. Championship Golf Services Inc
60. 18th hole
61. Towel, ___ bag
62. "Eager" to play
63. Betting term
64. Range currency
65. Southern Nationals Disc Golf
66. 2012 PGA Championship win, Mcilroy

Down

1. Winter golf conditions
2. "___ birdie!" (possessive)
3. Shed by pros after big win
4. Golf time-share meeting
5. Heated competition
6. NN - The Goose
7. Tees ___ balls
8. No power cart today
9. 1st time golfer
10. Snack shack nacho cheese
11. Injury, major side effect
12. ___ Trophy, biennial tourney
13. Cut from TOUR
21. First tee, for picture
23. World Golf Hall of Fame
28. HOF Judy Rankin
29. Common green shape
30. A Glove's making
31. Stylus control golf VG: Abbr
32. Balls to golf if club is gun
33. "Holes" in line of play
35. Complete miss, or ___ ball
38. HOF Amy Alcott, initially
39. Presidential golf Bill
40. Golf tourney structure
41. Sun off course dew
42. Solid piece of mud on clubhead
43. Masters Green Jacket needs
45. Food shack offerings
46. Club points left
49. Fan tribute to pro
50. Came up short
51. Fee for tournament
52. PGA HQ mtg, by ___ only: Abbr
53. 3 Golfer group
54. Golf website click-navigation
55. Pay to play, also poker
59. New "type" of player

PUZZLE 3

1	2	3	4		5	6	7	8		9	10	11	12	13

Golf Fact: Augusta National is the most famous golf club in the world

Across

1. Run one at the golf course bar
4. Cut, from tourney
7. Distance ball traveled after landing
9. Golf award show
10. HOF Retief Goosen
12. The crowd ___ after the long putt
13. Post round evening meal
15. Better rental clubs, same price
17. Printed coins of golf pros
18. Tallahassee Disc Golf Assoc.
19. Golf America Online Ent.
21. New course mng needed
22. Heavy putter head
24. There's bad balls in every case
25. 2, 4, 6, 8 Holes
26. Links plant-brush, gorse - ulex
28. NN - Crooner
30. Performance of expensive ball vs cheap
32. The player ___ anchor the club
35. Time to use bright balls
39. ___ hit until green is clear
40. Strange brew, served in course lounge
42. Downturn in gameplay
44. Hot golf market recently, continent
45. Stories of Tiger's greatness
46. "Fantastic 4" star & 200yd driver
47. Hole needs to go from 500y to 420y
49. Snack hut offers
52. Original disc, for frolf, was what?
53. Demeanor, when playing in a rhythm
54. HOF Ernie Els
55. Golfer Big Cat Williams, first
56. Quit golf club
57. Plastic club for kids

58. Tiger scandal news, fans ___ & feather

Down

1. Course's playing field
2. ESA - Environmental Sensitive ___
3. A teammate quickly becomes one
4. Caddyshack Ty Webb's known as
5. 1932 PGA Championship win, Dutra
6. Bill Rogers NN
7. PGA vs all other Tours
8. Pro shop negotiation
10. Chase - Caddyshack II reprisal
11. NN - Hubie, The Doberman
12. Players that don't improve, stay in these
14. Doesn't know the rules
16. European Golf Design
17. New equipment, yearly release
20. Looks over the course's books
23. Settles after controversy
27. First US Open, length of tourney
29. Barren course
31. "Golf's too complicated" says who?
32. 1800's wood shaft, iron-head, like 5-iron
33. Pro Golfer's assoc. is not one, like NFLPA
34. Katherine Hepburn as a golfer in the "Pat and Mike" golf movie
36. For safety in and out of power-cart
37. Hoot and ___ at a pro's success
38. Tiger considered Hogan's swing the one ___
39. Class of golfers
41. " ___ whiz my swing sucks"
43. Score from "yesterday's" round
48. Old school TV device to record golf tourney
50. 2 sing at course karaoke
51. International Pitch & Putt Assoc.

PUZZLE 4

Golf Fact: A golf ball has between 300 and 500 dimples

Across

1. Golfing keeps you ___ & hearty
5. Golf book of "things" (sl)
9. Abnormal Ground Conditions
12. Golf magazine passed around
13. Eases a golfer's sun burn
14. Heard during winter golf
16. Mad golfer
17. Blindside
18. Pros say to swing w it = success
19. Jerking club ___ power
20. Hole after the 9th
22. Tourney prices saw it, in 2021
23. Overseas made club arrive here first
24. Course walkers are usually
27. Modern Woods material, ___ fiber
29. All over the place golfer
31. Head cover material supplier (animal)
32. Player glows on the links
33. Q-school, will ___ your score claims
36. Toughen grip
37. Well hit ball will usually ___
39. Golf TV audio equipment, hi-___
40. 1980 "PGA Golf" videogame - ___ vision
41. Club play, golf partner change
45. Golfer mock their buddies swing
46. Hardpan lie, means shots hit ___
48. Cigar, for celebration (slang)
50. Golf times marked on calendar
52. Sun appears off course dew
53. Grant club use for the day, or a swing
56. Big grass divot (slang)
57. Barely used clubs
58. Round is "tied"
59. ___ Trophy, biennial tourney
60. Delete score
61. Ben Hogan, best in his (time)
62. Targeted by early disc golfer
63. "Emailed" the membership application

Down

1. Superb golfing
2. Farmlinks Golf Club locale
3. Bob hits, then Carl. "Carl"
4. Visor hider
5. Pulled on naive golfer
6. Membership addendum
7. Course reception
8. Tourney medical is under one
9. One's scoring should mimic Honest ___
10. Masters Jackets offer it to wearer
11. Craig Robert Stadler initially
12. Plush course grass
15. Autograph, not happening
21. Maraging steel clubs, vs all clubs
23. LPGA golfer Renee P.
25. Shot birdie, leader bogied
26. Golf apparel "set"
28. Disc golf putter characteristic
30. Health = Walk course & ___ portions
33. Famous Torrey ___ s Course, San Diego
34. $$ down on membership
35. Lost bet, need to pay
37. Tires on a golf cart, size
38. NN - Gene the Machine
39. Kids toy, now golf device
42. "Hanging" towel from bag
43. PGA TOUR stop and HTC phone-maker
44. Dutch Harrison first
47. Bad reaction, action to snack shack
49. Pro Robert Jones middle
51. Player's helper or caddie (short)
52. Mario Golf, super game system: Abbr
54. Night before golf
55. Talent is in their "genes"

PUZZLE 5

Golf Fact: Smaller golf balls of the past can travel further than today's larger balls

Across

1. Hardpan lie
5. Garcia, 2007 CA Champ. in cup
9. NN - Champagne Tony
10. Graeme McDowell NN
13. "All" leather gloves
14. Golfer Big Cat Williams, first
15. Findlay Area Golf Assoc.
16. Pay to play, also poker
17. Critters do to a course (3wd)
19. Caddy service
22. Cheerful course staff
23. Course beer option
24. Pebble Beach place (short)
25. Chinese tourney benefit
26. Sergio Garcia NN
27. Old Ladies Golf Assoc.
28. Club rentals may be sold as
30. White tee box markers
33. Course pro designer
36. Basket balls into range stall tray
39. Player messes up
42. Fan assigned
43. NN - Hound Dog
45. Real Time Golf
47. Golf TV, btw shows
48. Heard during winter golf
49. ___ to play golf (time of life)
51. GPS screen in cart
53. Power cart
54. Player injuries req.
55. Golf shirts & pants (short)
57. Cart path
58. Player bodies do it poorly
59. Heathland course common tree
60. Course Corp. structure: Abbr
61. Minus 1 golfer
62. Visor hider

Down

1. Evil golfer
2. Visualize ball into hole
3. Speed golfer round
4. Play through? Finger denial
5. Designated garage "area" for clubs
6. Hooligan golfer (slang)
7. Golf news source
8. Young golfer
9. PGA TOUR ___ Tiger in 2000s
10. Madden Esports official energy drink
11. Travelling tour need
12. Golden Tee VG housing
18. Hogan, golf swing "think"
20. Redeem your score
21. Course prefers you use plastic
23. A cart's speed governor function
27. Happy Gilmores caddy's name
29. Legend of Bagger Vance, Damon
31. Fill out scorecard
32. Lose the round
34. Ricky Fowler clubs
35. Marshal says to slow players
37. Excuse for using a cart
38. A golf cart's purpose
40. Residence near fairway
41. Gorse make-up
44. Delete score
46. Why golf son is great
48. God will to help your score
50. Scorecard total
52. Course top mng (short)
53. Ohio city course (short)
56. ___ tendo, Mario Golf

PUZZLE 6

	1	2	3			4			5	6	7	8	
9					10	11		12		13			
14					15					16			
17				18			19	20					21
22						23					24		
25				26						27			
	28		29			30			31				
32			33		34	35							
36	37	38							39		40	41	
42					43			44			45		46
47				48				49		50			
51			52				53						
	54					55	56				57		
	58				59					60			
	61								62				

Golf Fact: Caddie or Caddy come from the
French military word "cadet"

Across

1. At driving range, ___ for a stall
5. Less athletic golf bod
9. Golf cart seating type
14. Julius Boros NN
15. Sinks winning putt for team
16. Caddyshack, judge's first name
17. United States Golf Teachers
18. "Fantastic 4" star & 200yd driver
19. Event location e.g. course
20. Bad hole, happened again
22. Satsuki Club, famous 964 yard hole
24. Ball's outer shell
26. Farmlinks Golf Club northern locale
27. Can't do with a golf cart, for safety
30. Staying away from snack shack, reason
31. Extend membership
32. All scores "tallied up"
36. Pro golfer big-headed trait
37. Presser "___ was saying...", reminder
38. Sand hazard (slang)
43. Pro shop buy-all
47. Tattered golf clothes
48. John Daly's restaurant arrest
49. Golfers pin type, fashion
52. Turn body on backswing
53. Changed to the rules
55. Golf words
59. Driving range speed of shots
60. Sliced ball hits rock, damage result
62. Believes golf stories
63. Tee time before noon
64. 4-some comes together when they play
65. Ladies Southside Golf Assoc.
66. Longer than avg. putter
67. Nebraska Senior Golf Assoc.
68. Many monthly rounds fit in one

Down

1. Masters Green Jacket is the ___ & reward
2. 12 pack of balls
3. Asia Pacific Golf Confederation
4. Links course brush is vs manicured course
5. Pros repeat it on Dancing w the Stars
6. Pro is giving lessons
7. Frank "Fuzzy" Zoeller middle
8. CAN Weir's Master Dinner menu
9. Disc golf putter characteristic
10. Lessons, to your game
11. Front and back halves
12. Chili-dip, slang for what? (grass)
13. Golf shirt "coloring"
21. Player behind in car payments risks
23. Press reports what pro ___
25. Break a golf rule is one (holy)
27. Golf equipment "detail" sheet (short)
28. Three Rivers Golf Assoc.
29. Grounds crews battle this underground to surface golf-green wrecker
30. Driving Accuracy, stat
33. "Go for it"
34. United States Golf Register
35. Fruit pastry at concession
39. Black vs gold tee difference
40. Swing quickly, or range shot pace
41. Sonic and golf videogame maker, in reverse
42. HOF Patty Sheehan
43. Sun off course dew
44. TV camera angle: Abbr
45. Ticket sales produce it (slang)
46. "Wholly, completely" filled scorecard
50. Old clubs in for credit
51. Treated golf clothing does if wet
52. Sport shirts for golfers
54. Golf book legal ID: Abbr
56. Play "fake"
57. Myrtle Beach Golf Assoc.
58. Course BBQ cooking, just the outside
59. Poke fun at golfer's play style
61. Thomas Dickson Armour initials

PUZZLE 7

1	2	3	4		5	6	7	8		9	10	11	12	13
14					15						16				
17					18						19				
20				21		22			23						
		24		25				26					
27	28	29					30							
31							32				33	34	35
36											37			
38			39	40	41	42		43	44	45	46		
			47				48						
49	50	51				52								
	53					54				55		56	57	58
59					60			61		62				
63					64						65		
66					67						68		

Golf Fact: Over 300 million golf balls are lost every year in the United States

Across

1. Bad hole, happened again
6. Aggie Legends Golf Classic
10. American Singles Golf Assoc.
14. Pros and The Green Jacket
15. Undesirable score
16. PGA Championship
17. Medieval golf group
18. PGA hedging, insur ___
19. Shop with used golf equipment
20. Original term for "chunk"
22. Course, federal regulation area & marker
24. Real golfers "put up with" any weather
26. Pro Bobby Jones NN
29. Covers the course
34. Golf website, Search Engine Optimization
35. Home of the famous Blue Monster course
38. Pro Robert Cruickshank's middle
39. Teardrop Golf Co. on Nasdaq
41. Green design with center as high point
43. Standard golf "Look out" warning
44. Old moth ___ golf clothes
46. Forced carry obstacle type
48. Nebraska Golf Assoc.
49. Upcoming PGA events "schedule"
50. Mini golf in early 20th C.
52. "Rocky" loves golf
56. Affluent golfer (3wd)
60. United PGA place
64. "Spot" or division of any hole
65. Rhode Island Golf Assoc.
67. Stand place, while opp. is hitting (courtesy)
68. Cups edges
69. Cart noise (comical)
70. Resort golf clubhouse (cabin-like)
71. Course requires your golf attire to be
72. Player's helper or caddy (short)
73. Food carried in bag

Down

1. Tattered golf clothes
2. Lessons purpose, i.e. to learn (short)
3. Golf shoe-lace looping
4. 9:00, but tee-time was 8:46 (slang)
5. Legend of Bagger Vance Dir. Robert
6. Triumphant saying, figuring out swing prob.
7. Molding in the cart's rear, for bags
8. Georgia Golf Course Super. Assoc.
9. Everyone does it (dishonestly)
10. Tee-time is this at a course, essentially (short)
11. Seniors' Golf Assoc. of Arkansas
12. Fans stop and do at god-like pro
13. Junior or teen golfer problem
21. Unplayable wet weather / course cond.
23. Sonic maker & fr. pub. of golf videogames
25. Reason for an X-out on a golf ball
26. Which pro has the NN - Robopro
27. Amateur tourney prize, same as Olympics
28. Mobile course potty
30. Raymond Loran Floyd initially
31. Course request, drive carts ___ the path
32. Pro Orville Moody NN
33. Pro with the NN - Old Baldy
36. Master's winner asks " ___ dreaming?"
37. Ranges are a stack or multi what?
40. Golf's many etiquettes, AKA ___ peeves
42. Barely used course / trial clubs
45. Course critter home
47. Barely used course owned clubs
51. Needed if canceling on your 4-some
53. Pro with the NN - Toy Tiger
54. Chi-Chi's goodbye to golf
55. Sponsor IDs
56. Marshal will to rule breaker
57. Cleveland course water neighbor
58. Pro with the NN - Champagne Tony
59. 18th hole
61. Tiger Woods mother (short)
62. European Disc Golf Championship
63. Lost ball action
66. Touring pro earnings, can be high ___: Abbr

PUZZLE 8

1	2	3	4	5		6	7	8	9		10	11	12	13
14						15					16			
17						18					19			
20					21		22			23				
			24			25								
26	27	28							29	30	31	32	33
34				35			36	37	38				
39			40		41				42		43			
44			45		46					47		48		
49							50			51			
			52	53	54	55							
56	57	58	59					60			61	62	63
64					65		66		67			
68					69				70			
71					72				73			

Golf Fact: "Lefty" Mickelson is actually right-handed

Across

1. Done to bug swarms on course
5. "Cunning" golf strategy
11. Golfer will at green, pre putt
12. Increase, strengthen grip
14. 2 before 13th
15. Birdie on a 4 ___ you a 3
16. Won tourney back-to-back
17. PGA TOUR Par 4 ace in 2001, M___
18. Play golf in the snow?
19. Lateral hazard stake
20. Terrible, bottom-end golfers (slang)
21. Achieve your best score
22. Modern driver head shape, kinda
24. Ladies Amateur Golf Assoc.
25. Arrange tee-off order
26. Mulligan
27. Older player hair color
28. Golfer verbiage after a slice
29. Tee-box hit per hole
31. Early metal driver face plate
32. Scoring well demeanor
34. Average driver distance is 226 yards
35. Scrambling stat (short)
39. Up and ___ the tree
40. Excited fans ___ over the Pro
41. Golf equipment, e.g. club
42. Cart (slang)
43. Associations must play ball with (short)
44. Popular pro player's attorneys' org.: Abbr
45. Estimated Energy Requirement (to e.g. golf)
46. Round is over, missing, never again
47. Jess to Nelly, Korda (LPGA)
50. When a cart is in your way
52. Wanna be pro golfers, yearn, want, dream...
53. Golf bag AKA, for clubs not clothes
54. Temp tee marker
55. Missed hit reaction from rest of 4-some
56. "Best Colonel Bogey" is a what?

Down

1. Golf w mom's hubby
2. Play-through, or safe-to-hit signal
3. Course marked - Environmental Sensitive ___
4. Golf tourney structure
5. Tiger as a cheater, on spouse
6. 18 on a typical course
7. Golf law
8. Ball (slang)
9. Tourney "___ and Winners"
10. Play different today
11. Golf shirt short design for cool conditions
13. In line to tee-off
14. Scorecard miscalculation
15. PGA CEO Seth
20. Bag's bottom
21. Common ball eater
23. "Smashed" on booze during round
24. Caddyshack, Judge Smails hot niece
25. Sunscreen reason
28. Cart parking stall blocker
30. Writer of PGA News: Abbr
31. Golf gambles, placed for money
32. Ball goes into cup
33. 3-star course rating
34. Young Daly's family did it a lot, transient
36. First metal clubs had a wood ___
37. Craig Stadler's middle
38. Sunglasses ease it during round
40. "Showed off" new golf shirt
42. Seagle Electronic Golf Library
43. Ball hits tree, likely result
46. Replacement golfer,"Jim will ___ me"
47. Take advantage of "naive" golfers
48. Pro golfer Aoki
49. It's put on the ball for direction
51. Richmond Golf Assoc.

PUZZLE 9

Golf Fact: At 14,335 ft above sea level, the Tactu Golf Club in Peru is the highest altitude course in the world

Across

1. Courses lounges AKA
5. Rory and Tiger shine
9. Pro Jan Stephenson NN
13. "$10 you won't make par"
14. Early tourney cuts ___ earn any $
15. Plays in Pro-Am with pro golfer
16. Clubhouse fancy pants event
17. Double birdie AKA
18. Favorite club
19. Fashionable golf attire
21. Davis Love III NN
23. Cleveland course water neighbor
24. Flying high over score
25. College Golf Fellowship
28. No-go summer footwear for golf
30. Barren course
32. Thomas Dickson Armour, initially
33. Won tourney back-to-back
37. Speed golfer round
39. Decipher numbers to get score
40. Absorb tourney coverage
42. Famous Old Tokyo course, tourney locale
45. The Golf Improvement Center
46. Tee off honors go ___
48. Older player hair color
49. Warp, or lasting damage of club
51. Nintendo golf videogame super console: Abbr
54. Women's equivalent to Ryder Cup
55. Tourney grandstand seating area
59. Don't drive power-cart ___ the green
60. Course grass leveller
62. Caddyshack's Chase as Ty
63. " ___ in the win", like fishing
64. Early metal driver face plate
65. "Team" play
66. Pro Robert Jones middle
67. Tourney medical is under this temp. structure
68. Double digits scores, doubles of par 5s

Down

1. Holds equipment and accessories
2. ___ to MLB as "a club" is to PGA
3. Use / lean on favorite club over and over
4. Old golf shoes, like old bread
5. Play-through request answer (positive)
6. PGA broadcast language (short)
7. Power-cart plastic body parts
8. Outstanding, star-filled game
9. Clubhouse lounge, late place to be
10. Pros compassion for The Green Jacket
11. PGA vs all other Tours
12. Eases sun burn from a round of golf
14. Quit the game of golf, no longer play
20. Iron club (short)
22. ESPN golf documentary, a telling of what?
25. Power, push or pull
26. Golf Range Assoc. of America
27. Told all about your golf cheating
29. Some golfer's "person"alized drivers
31. Barely made putt (slang) (3wd)
34. Environmental Leaders in Golf Awards
35. Pro Payne Stewart's NN
36. Aid built into clubs (short)
38. Players visor shade / color design
41. Disc golf, # of discs in bag rule
43. Sweets at snack shack
44. Cranky old golfer
47. Debris in your line, OK to ___
49. Skins game prize
50. Golf membership addendum
52. European Cup
53. Walk w confidence, after big hit
54. Scorecard box-row info...a numeric what?
56. Golf Digest Best of, Castle Oaks in ___ CA
57. 1932 PGA Championship win, Dutra
58. Range catchers
61. Match play, most holes ___

PUZZLE 10

Golf Fact: Balls travel further in summer because of less dense air

Across

1. Old Scot golf group
5. Golfer (JPN) pro, Aoki
9. Range finder helps
14. Colonial C.C., Hogan's course
15. Driving range, for a stall
16. 10am, but tee-time was 9:32
17. "Without a Trace" CBS star, avid golfer
19. Course operations at night
20. ESA stakes jurisdiction
21. Amsterdam's Crusaders nickname
23. Early round energy (UK)
24. Ball down fairway, like mail
25. Playing from the Pros (tee)
27. Golf tourney grouping example
30. Putt longer than flag stick, betting, game
31. Rewarded golfer, based on it
32. Out of cart fumble
33. Sawbill Frisbee Golf Assoc.
37. Mulligan shot,from scoring
38. Not permitted during round
39. Tourney RSVP pressure
40. Course open during winter?
41. Tin Cup, female lead Russo
42. Power cart base
43. Indoor putting carpet
45. Prepared to play
46. Cart brake noise, may need repair
49. Ball into water hazard, sound
50. Player's repeat it competing on DWTS
51. PGA top exec: Abbr
52. Barely used course clubs
56. Ball washer finish
58. Same course, same score
60. Cold, clammy handed golfer
61. Course access number
62. Tee box hit per hole
63. Low & Slow AKA One ___ Takeaway
64. Straight, flat hole difficulty rating
65. Course requirement

Down

1. Course foody
2. Story of Tiger's greatness
3. Surrounded by e.g. golfers
4. Need clubs, balls and beers
5. Tiger's home Jupiter ___ , FL
6. Marshal to rowdy player
7. Tourney crowds radio batteries
8. Putters only on green rule
9. Carts locked up at night
10. Game time player mood
11. Part of course drainage filter
12. Club and cleat washing equip.
13. Snack shack offering
18. Fairway high point
22. Craig Wood's (Pro golfer's) middle
26. Check the club's tag for "details"
27. Keep up w the play (saying)
28. NN is Champagne Tony
29. Barren course
30. Joke pulled on golf partner
32. A wood, likely 1 at this time
34. "#1" finger
35. Golfing is classified as one
36. "Cut" from tour
38. Steps to find lost club, also a draw type
42. 9 ___ and 9-back
44. Keep playing badly, for a while now
45. Rookie golfer, ball loss #s
46. "Cancel" tourney
47. Short "spicy" shot - ___ dip (slang)
48. A driving type
49. Pro-Am'er, non pro golfer
53. Junior golfer sweat gland problem
54. Golf shoe tie
55. Cart (slang)
57. Pros quotes are actual
59. Most hackers tourney life hopes: Abbr

PUZZLE 11

1	2	3	4		5	6	7	8		9	10	11	12	13
14					15					16				
17				18						19				
20							21	22				23		
			24				25			26				
27	28	29				30								
31					32					33	34	35	36	
37				38						39				
40				41					42					
			43	44				45						
46	47	40					49							
50				51			52				53	54	55	
56			57		58	59					62			
60					61					62				
63					64					65				

Golf Fact: A golfer has a 1 in 12,500 chance of hitting a hole-in-one

Across

1. Express annoyance at bad shot
5. Players faces on TV HUD
9. Pros Goalby & Gilder
13. Methodical player
14. No frills swing
15. Cleveland course water neighbor
16. Tiger Woods mother (short)
17. Turf type for hitting balls
18. National Amputee Golf Assoc.
19. 1989 PGA Championship win
21. Course "varmint"
23. Post game Japanese course bevy
24. Dog part shaped hole
25. Victory speech sound booster (short)
28. Pro Bobby Jones NN
30. Balls into range machine
32. Wins add to a golfers what? :Abbr
33. United PGA place
37. Membership addendum, also tailor duty
39. Stand here, while another is hitting
40. Tee orders seem to each hole, back n forth
42. Ryder Cup reserve players
45. Sonic maker & fr. publisher of golf games
46. Masters time
48. Snead slang, "Play it Again, ___ "
49. Caddyshack, Danny's girlfriend
51. They can afford to golf
54. Pro James Ferrier's middle
55. Happy Gilmore, Shooter
59. International Disc Golf Assoc.
60. Angered golfer
62. Pro has a memorable one to fans
63. Abandoned when at snack shack
64. PGA is the one vs all other Tours
65. Delaware State Golf Assoc.
66. Course owner changes with this
67. "Elation" from round win, also TV dance show
68. Cushion in power-cart

Down

1. Popular store merchandise
2. Golf team AKA
3. Lower speed, end of ball flight
4. Game OK, but putting and chip bad
5. Golf, a popular one for many
6. Title___ brand balls and equipment
7. Cart goes round & round. Also ball shape
8. Course card documenters
9. Bowed grass strain
10. Golf TV hosts job
11. Pro Ed Dudley NN
12. Course BBQ cooking
14. Happy Gilmore, played himself - Bob
20. HOF Amy Alcott, initially
22. "___ birdie!" (possessive)
25. "I tried but ___, I lost"
26. Course damaging critter
27. Pro's NN - Volcano
29. Putts per greens in regulation
31. Cart driver assignment
34. Rare results across entire foursomes
35. Edmonton Disc Golf Assoc.
36. Golf shirt stitches
38. A driving type
41. Slow group causes
43. Make shift divot repair tool
44. Bad golf shots & most bread
47. Cart fuel, UK
49. Ruthless to slumping pro
50. Holy course investor
52. Callaway Golf
53. Too much "wrist" in putts
54. Tourney auction actions
56. Fairway Elm tree shape
57. Ironwood Men's Golf Assoc.
58. Club requires golf attire to be
61. Consumed, at snack shack

PUZZLE 12

Golf Fact: The world's longest hole is the 7th hole, 964 yard Par-7 at Satsuki Golf Club in Japan

Across

1. Course owner land possession
5. Missed cut, ___ has sailed
9. Golfer tries to ___ the tourney standing
14. Push carts "lessen" back pain from carrying
15. Ladies Amateur Golf Assoc.
16. Putt longer than flag stick, betting game
17. Targets, stat: Abbr
18. Major injuries, rush to emerg ___
19. Hole ___, means 1 one the scorecard
20. Players access to HOF
22. Golf is a light form of it
24. Guarantee a tee time
25. Golf is "entertainment" (short)
26. At least one club to play round
27. Expand hole by yardage
32. Schedules are full of them (numbers)
34. Cart ID number
35. PED testing place
36. Blocked shot, from obstacle-object (short)
37. DNF from tourney, with ___
41. Early or old-time club metal face-plate
44. Exit routine, to golf and relax. Also back-up
46. Tee-time, period. Also a gambling machine
47. First Olympics for golf since 1904
48. Physically-able to golf
52. Golf, became more ___ popular in the 2000s
56. Rare long iron, hard to hit
57. Balls into driving range machines, actions
58. Yappy golfer told to put "one" in it
60. 18th hole
61. Popular format bingo-bango- ___
62. PGA TOUR Par 4 ace in 2001
63. Betting term
64. Pro Miguel Jimenez's middle
65. 3 holes of a full 18
66. Pro golfer McIlroy

Down

1. Caddy's caution
2. Double birdie AKA
3. Pro NN - Robopro
4. Father to son golfers
5. 3-pack golf ball package
6. Cross method of holding putter
7. International Golf Corp.
8. Pro shop visit purpose
9. Ranting player discharge
10. NE state with pretty courses (short)
11. Eases sunny round's burn
12. Cinematic game capture (camera)
13. Visor hider
21. Targeted by early disc golfer
23. TOUR player accommodations type
28. HOF Allan Robertson
29. Tailgate BBQ rack of
30. Players wives
31. CAN Weir's Master Dinner menu
32. Go-for-it or are you chicken?
33. ___ is to MLB as "a club" is to PGA
35. Tourney Leader (short)
38. World Record score (short)
39. He sprays the ball (slang)
40. Watch golf in man-cave / hideaway
41. Range completely covered in balls appearance
42. Low budget cart path liner/railings
43. Masters Green Jacket fitted by
45. Golf shoe toe area top
46. Fills out scorecard
49. Fan tribute to pro. Also well-known cable ch.
50. Not a winner
51. ___ fee for tournament
52. "Fantastic 4" star & 200yd driver
53. Mid round time est.
54. Messed up shot, reaction
55. Michigan Disc Golf Empire
59. Oklahoma Golf Assoc.

PUZZLE 13

Golf Fact: Tiger's estimated net worth is over $800 Million USD

Across

1. Mid-range golf disc
4. General (golf) friend, greeting
7. Club stays on ground longer, contact
9. LPGA golfer Heather F.
10. N.Y. area courses, in the US: Abbr
12. Uppity golfer talks down to caddy
13. Pro with the NN - The Missouri Mortician
15. Makes up an iron
17. Featherie - old ball material
18. Happy Gilmore actor, Sandler
19. Golf shirts & pants if they were standard PGA (short)
21. Player's growing list of things
22. Scorecard extras scribbled down
24. Fide type golf star
25. Records are for best ___
26. Reports on golf
28. Steady slow swing is "wanted"
30. Feeling after a long, wet round
32. Golf Channel's satellite provider
35. To hit ball w club bottom
39. Maraging in clubs, also in ___
40. ___ and holler at pro's success
42. Long Putters current status
44. Barely ___ out the win
45. Bad luck - ball lands then veers ___ hazard
46. Charity tourney for cancer ___
47. Heckler does it to pro
49. Sleeve for golf balls
52. Most do this with gloves when putting
53. Golfing single, becomes a groups 4th
54. HOF Davis Love III
55. They like to golf and have the money to do it
56. Pro golfer Natalie Gulbis NN
57. Pro contracts, not exact. (short)
58. Rec Sport Golf

Down

1. One day, many golf lessons
2. Course dues, amount AKA
3. A Majors tourney
4. Driver, irons, putter (3wd)
5. "Spot" on hole
6. Course damager
7. When pros shooting over par
8. "Design" a course from scratch
10. Clubs, balls and beers...for a great day
11. Scorecard miscalculation
12. Ball to the head
14. Balls into pocket
16. Where to soak dirty clubs
17. Early clubs shaft-to-head joiner thread
20. Hit the ball "cleanly"
23. Cart parking, over there to the ___
27. Professional designer of golf courses
29. Nicklaus is for Daly
31. Redeem your score
32. 1929 PGA Championship win
33. Pro golfer NN - Inky
34. Course revamp
36. Top ten order of golfers (chicken)
37. Tropical course critter
38. Shoot par
39. Dustin Johnston often sports it
41. PGA TOUR among all tours
43. Golfer will at his competition to intimidate
48. Pro Payne Stewart's NN
50. Knocked out ball
51. Golf camp cheap beds

PUZZLE 14

Golf Fact: Celine Dion owns the Le Mirage Golf Club in Quebec

Across

1. Post round stomach desires
5. Grass chunk. Also nacho cheese pile
9. HOF pro A.W. Tillinghast
12. Caddyshack's Gopher, during credit roll
13. Golf Digest's Best in '94 - Castle Oaks Golf Club, ___ N. California
14. Golf data type
16. American Soc. of Golf Course Arch.
17. Cart (slang)
18. Scottish Blind Golf Society
19. 2003 PGA Championship win, Micheel
20. Hole #1
22. Team victory all-around action
23. The Justin of the PGA
24. Course walkers are usually
27. Uses to watch golf match (sl)
29. All over the place golfer
31. Compile, scores
32. Never-use club
33. Result
36. Mock and ridicule buddies swing
37. Range covered in balls, like a warm ___
39. Wilderness course animal, Bob ___
40. PGA TV slot
41. Watch and ___ during golf lesson
45. Early golf days, high-loft wood club
46. Course needs $ + a strong ___ to survive (short)
48. Aces
50. Why your son is great at golf
52. Legendary pro's NN - Bantam Ben
53. Sportswriter double-check
56. Wind force, not suitable for golfing
57. Bond items to bag
58. NFL Titans golf here on summer break (short)
59. PGA TOUR Champions, ___ 50 and older
60. Caddyshack movie's dialogue exchange
61. Hit the ball "chunk"
62. A Tour's biggest problem, why many fold
63. "Eager" to play

Down

1. Random golfers in a 4-some
2. Jerk club = Shoulders fail to ___
3. Did you choke on purpose?
4. Younger golfer, fat-free body type
5. Pro Henry Picard's middle
6. Pro Justin Thomas' middle
7. Flag and cup location
8. Course stingers
9. West Coast golf tourney broadcast starts
10. All the pro e-stats are here
11. Tee-To-Green
12. Done during speed golf, quickly
15. Putting is main ___ of mini golf
21. Flags, function
23. Course fee coupon action
25. Clubhouse fancy-pants event
26. Golf hat sharing risk
28. Auto storage at course
30. Pro must win on occasion to ___ pro card
33. Wet course risk
34. 1st mini golf location - North ___
35. Don't drive the power-cart ___ the green
37. Range balls holder
38. Young golfer
39. To-the-pin rule (KP)
42. Canadian $, ball marker
43. A cart go'er
44. PGA needs to "clean-up" their rules
47. Half of pro-am participation (short)
49. Mario Golf's Super console: Abbr
51. Surprise reaction to green fee increase
52. DeChambeau if Marvel character
54. Lay-up type of move (short)
55. Explosive golfer nickname

PUZZLE 15

Golf Fact: Amateur Richard Lewis golfed 600 rounds in a single year. He walked 2500 miles and took 50,000 shots in 2010

Across

1. Players are to a tour wheel
5. "Spot" on hole
9. Said of a ball hit into thick trees
10. Hot golf market, continent
13. West Australian Golf League
14. "Elation" from round win. Also dancing TV show
15. Golf glove AKA
16. Assoc. of Swiss Golf Managers
17. Courses without golfers
19. Golfer w head in clouds
22. Double bogeys on fives
23. Course diet-beer option
24. Talent is in their "genes"
25. Synonym for hole-in-one
26. Negative Tiger news, purpose
27. Tiger is top contender for all-time status: Abbr
28. Golf course obstacle
30. Begin playing
33. Choking, funny golfer
36. Putting area, if close enough
39. Game day ___ sion
42. Fans for hometown player
43. Best nines AKA
45. Last hole
47. Oregon Golf Review
48. Play "fake"
49. Study/ look over the rule, briefly
51. Pro's NN - Willie the Wedge
53. Tight fit, a fight to get clubs from bag
54. Grass is vs turf is not
55. Quit the club game in 2016
57. In shoes after trap shot
58. Environmental Leaders in Golf Awards
59. Changes in game momentum, often (water ref)
60. Course trash holders
61. Attack-kill the ball, like it's a dragon
62. This wind type really alters ball flight

Down

1. Driving-range tractor action
2. Bogey, to a golfer
3. Pond wildlife
4. Golf outfit, UK
5. Good caddies are "alert", of course
6. Sweaty golf clothes rub result
7. Half-cracked golfer, is ___ by other golfers
8. Like a golf history book
9. Georgia Golf Course Superintendent Assoc.
10. Bill Murray is known to at the Pro-ams
11. Course lounge high-ball action
12. Masters Green Jacket needs before awarding
18. $ tours, the best pros
20. A golf bag carries them
21. Numbers for golf times marked on calendar
23. Power-cart use certification
27. Great dads pass on the golf one
29. Elderly Gentlemens' Golf Society
31. Partial membership payment
32. Caddyshack's gopher puppet
34. Links brush gorse - ulex (flowering)
35. Rural golfer class
37. Best pros make up to eight ___
38. Pro's NN - The Gentleman
40. "Golf" news show on Golf Channel
41. Uphill AKA
44. Course membership terms are OK
46. Tourney details (slang)
48. Golf TV broadcast signal
50. American Soc. of Golf Course Architects
52. National Amputee Golf Association
53. PGA Championship happens the ___ prior to Memorial Day: Abbr
56. Hole i, ii, ___

PUZZLE 16

Golf Fact: The winning golfer actually golf's the least (shots)

Across

1. Clubhouse vegan option
5. Great play or player (urban slang)
9. American Soc. of Golf Course Arch.
14. Tiger's ex
15. Terrible player needs his magic
16. Pigeon says you cheated
17. Quadruple bogey on a 5
18. Longshore Women's Golf Assoc.
19. Brand name on ball
20. Golf great Sam
22. Glove location, most common
24. Driving range - shots taken speed
26. Golfers towel may ___ his bag
27. To shallow out club on downswing
30. Golf ball descriptor, and a smooth head
31. Caddyshack, funniest golf movie ever?
32. Caddyshack's "I'm Alright"
36. Seen on female fan
37. Caffeine bevy, UK course
38. Legally, OK to putt with
43. Negative course rating
47. Big guy on team
48. Winner-winner, chicken dinner
49. Leave the golf course
52. Early golf - a clubhouse used to be "big home"
53. Pro's image on tourney promo
55. Caddyshack's Smails claims "I ___ slice"
59. Angered golfer
60. Press report what pro ___
62. Turns often during an exciting match
63. Not a winner
64. Atmospheric condition, tough to see ball land
65. Golf puzzle book has many a
66. Fee type for tournament
67. Players visor 'block' design
68. Oh, ___ I missed (non-curse)

Down

1. Lowest double digit scores on a hole
2. 1932 PGA Championship win, Dutra
3. PGA's financial penalty
4. Discover buried lost ball
5. Davis Milton Love III, initially
6. First winner of US Open
7. A cracked ball
8. Didn't hear "FORE!"
9. Cart path black stuff
10. Links course Gorse brush make-up
11. Power-cart gets, when gas pedal pressed
12. Golf course rental place
13. Fill in golfer (short)
21. Stats
23. Tiger's mother's heritage
25. Course walkers are full of
27. Filipino Professional Golf Assoc.
28. Younger, healthy golfer body type
29. These bases have many courses
30. HOF pro Bob Harlow
33. Happy Gilmore's caddy's name
34. Ball by other ball
35. 1962 PGA Championship winner, Player
39. Tee time reservation, a form of
40. Same odds as becoming pro golfer
41. Writes an online course/club review
42. Ball Striking, stat
43. Fan compliment to pro, sometimes standing
44. ___ tendo's Mario Golf
45. Courses need $ + strong ___ to survive (short)
46. Glove give
50. Similar to a fringe
51. PGA Tour's "West ___ Swing"
52. FL golf hotspot
54. Player's caddy (short)
56. Spread "nasty, sleazy" rumor about pro
57. Lessons purpose (short)
58. Stinky old golf shoes
59. Ball in flight is a project ___
61. "Digital", golf tracker: Abbr

PUZZLE 17

1	2	3	4		5	6	7	8		9	10	11	12	13

Golf Fact: After a 112 year hiatus, Golf returned to the Olympics in 2016 (Rio)

Across

1. Golf trivia failure
6. Good Government Golf Tourney
10. National Anthem, pre tourney
14. Golf course clubhouse used to be "big home"
15. Hogan's intimidation feel
16. Course rule adherence
17. Scorecard is to a course
18. Golfer does over small hazard
19. Golf cart engine location
20. To "sign" your scorecard
22. Pre wedding golf event
24. Playing from reds, distance
26. Pulled on naive golfer
29. Tourney category, also those of age
34. Richmond Golf Association
35. Players visor design
38. Arnold Palmer NN
39. Golf glove rub
41. Lay-up = short of what full shot ___ reach
43. Credit sponsor of tourneys
44. Definitely not golf weather (cold)
46. Press "mixes" things up with controversies
48. Tiger scandal news, fans ___ & feather
49. Pushed to their limits golfer demeanor
50. Inheriting golf partner
52. Golf time-share pitch, meant to ___
56. Alluring golfer
60. Quit the game, leave the course
64. ESA - Environmental Sensitive ___
65. Pro Gene Littler's middle
67. Pro Helen Alfredsson's NN
68. Full cart going uphill "stops"
69. "Emailed" the membership
70. Tease friend about their tatter appearance
71. Barely ___ out the win
72. Visor hider
73. Pro Hubert Green's middle

Down

1. Salute Military Golf Association
2. Too-tight golf shirt
3. "Group" of golfers
4. Most pro golfers display "unassuming" demeanor
5. Steps prepping for stroke
6. Player's girlfriend
7. Member pays less for green fee than
8. Part of course drainage filter
9. Tournament luxury box food offering
10. Post game worn out, aching feeling
11. Made on a game by gamblers
12. Un-mixed drink in club lounge
13. Ball "spiral"
21. Liquid from concession, goes with gin
23. Golf Tourney Association of America
25. Course redos (short)
26. Pro's NN - Frosty
27. Course walkers are usually
28. Golf equipment ___ slump in winter
30. Golf Driver: Abbr
31. Golf teammates come together
32. LPGA - Walters & Hall
33. Shed by pros after big win
36. Club selection influenced by it the most
37. Caddyshack's Judge Smail's first name
40. Club collection
42. Feeling when shooting towards water, and then losing sight of ball
45. E-scorecard input
47. Disc golf flick shot
51. GolfTV shows game again
53. Delete score
54. Pro's NN - Radar
55. "___ is set for The Masters", famous line
56. Said when achieving score "I ___ par"
57. Northern Ohio course water neighbor
58. Lost ball action
59. Measurement of driver's large & heavy head
61. Alumni and Fan Golf Association
62. Violent laugh after golf joke
63. Tourney medical is under this portable obj.
66. Tourney earnings = dollars and ___ (short)

PUZZLE 18

Golf Fact: There are over 34,000 courses worldwide

Across

1. Club smack ball, noise
5. Mini golf first played here
11. NW USA course wildlife
12. Young golfer
14. Canadian $$, ball marker
15. Bag w supports
16. $ tours "attract" the best pros
17. Old course manager leaves, ___ a new one
18. Tourney "fix" is in. Also a huge truck
19. Defeat by a narrow margin
20. Courses lounges AKA
21. Cinematic game capture (camera)
22. Toss into divot
24. Slow golf can become a real ___
25. Rival golfers battles
26. Extreme Disc Golf Experience
27. Ace
28. Par is ___ 70 for US Open, usually
29. Clubs are "manufactured"
31. Course Mickeys
32. Claims many aces, no witness
34. Course fee AKA ___ 1
35. Scrambling, stat: Abbr
39. Water hazard plant life
40. A ball into soft sand trap will
41. Club to a golfer like a hammer to a carpenter
42. Golf ball is set-up
43. Burn Center Golf Invitational
44. Other baller type, league
45. Dead-F'in-Last: Abbr (slang)
46. "Story" of Tiger's greatness
47. Sour golfer
50. Last hole "saved" my handicap
52. Attach towel to bag
53. Tiger to his father
54. Burnt out club
55. Daly, over 300yd drives all ___
56. When a ball hits rock, possibility

Down

1. Tee off starter
2. Players do with their skills, over time
3. Hot golf market, continent
4. Teammate AKA
5. "Clothes" worn on course
6. Hazards and traps, to golfers
7. Tin Cup, female lead Russo
8. Mid-west courses west of Ohio (short)
9. Pro NN - El Pato (The Duck)
10. Team versus another
11. Rich golfer
13. Clubhouse breakfast
14. Last hole & all tied, aura
15. Membership sale %. Also, 1 unit of stock
20. Club-face of some 19th century clubs
21. "Newest" club fad, like this season's fashion
23. Tried out clubs before buying
24. Twists during swing
25. Pro William Earl Casper, initially
28. Weather resist shirt, smooth as ___ feel
30. Shots ___ penalties both count
31. Small course for putts
32. WMF use of "minigolf" vs miniature
33. Head weight is toward club's ___ & ___
34. Pro Ed Dudley's NN
36. PGA "event"
37. Pro Craig Stadler's middle
38. Sunglasses ease it during round
40. On the cart GPS device
42. TearDrop Golf Company
43. Popular format Bingo Bango ___
46. Untruths about his play
47. Clubs to PGA, ___ to MLB
48. Plays in Pro-Am and American contestant show
49. Tiger's mother's heritage
51. Trash talkers, never ___ loss for words

PUZZLE 19

Golf Fact: The world's oldest golf course is "The Old Course" at St. Andrews in Scotland

Across

1. Pro NN - Brillo
5. Horizontal AKA ___ swing plane
9. Done with Augusta prize
13. Mood of round loser (slang)
14. May redden during summer round
15. International Assoc. of Golf Admin.
16. Rewarded from tourney win
17. Golf to ___ money for charity
18. Scottish Golf Environment Group
19. Wager 1-off
21. Off-color, dirty golf joke
23. Didn't win
24. Press talk about tourney
25. Australian Golf Digest
28. Picked ___ spot for a lay-up shot
30. Opposite of bad golfer
32. Presser start - "___ questions?"
33. Ball dimples - "combat" wind
37. Sign - "No spikes upon ___ ", and door sign
39. Molding in the cart's rear, for bags
40. Back n forth tee order, also playground obj.
42. "The Big Easy" golfer
45. Northern Nevada Golf Assoc.
46. Masters is played when?
48. TV hosts ___ what is happening
49. Caddyshack movie, Danny's girlfriend
51. Air ball
54. Pro James Ferrier's middle
55. Winter golf course condition
59. Edmonton Disc Golf Assoc.
60. Angered golfer
62. EAS - Environmental Sensitive ___
63. John Daly's Coke of choice
64. PGA is the one vs all other Tours
65. High-sounding, club brand
66. Course owner will change if course is up for what?
67. Shooting well, mood. Also, trash bag brand
68. Collection of golf clubs

Down

1. Concession beer servers
2. Women Golf Assoc. of India
3. Barren course
4. Course wildlife singing
5. Use putter to ___ green's bumps
6. Worn on Maui course
7. "Classify" the various players
8. Nicklaus NN, not golden
9. The American Club famous mid-west course & Green Bay Packers state
10. Anxious to play
11. HOF McCormack, non player
12. Mad golfers turns hulk
14. Caddyshack movie, Judge Smails soda of choice
20. Buick Open
22. Starter's speech
25. PGA TOUR Champions = ___ 50 and older
26. LPGA's very own HOF, status
27. Fans fawn and ___ over the Pros
29. Well known match play cup
31. Cart driver assignment
34. Touring player accommodations
35. Fr. publisher of Virtua Golf videogame series
36. Range ball holder
38. A golf driving type
41. Slow group causes
43. Club's non members experience
44. Golf shots & most bread
47. Cart fuel, UK
49. Reports on the pros and tourney results
50. Holy course investor
52. Stroke Index, stat
53. Bag cover on-off'ers, makes noise
54. SleepNumber, official ___ of golf tourneys
56. Cleveland course water neighbor
57. "Emailed" the membership
58. Golfer's big gut, when he bends forward
61. Trash talkers, never ___ loss for words

PUZZLE 20

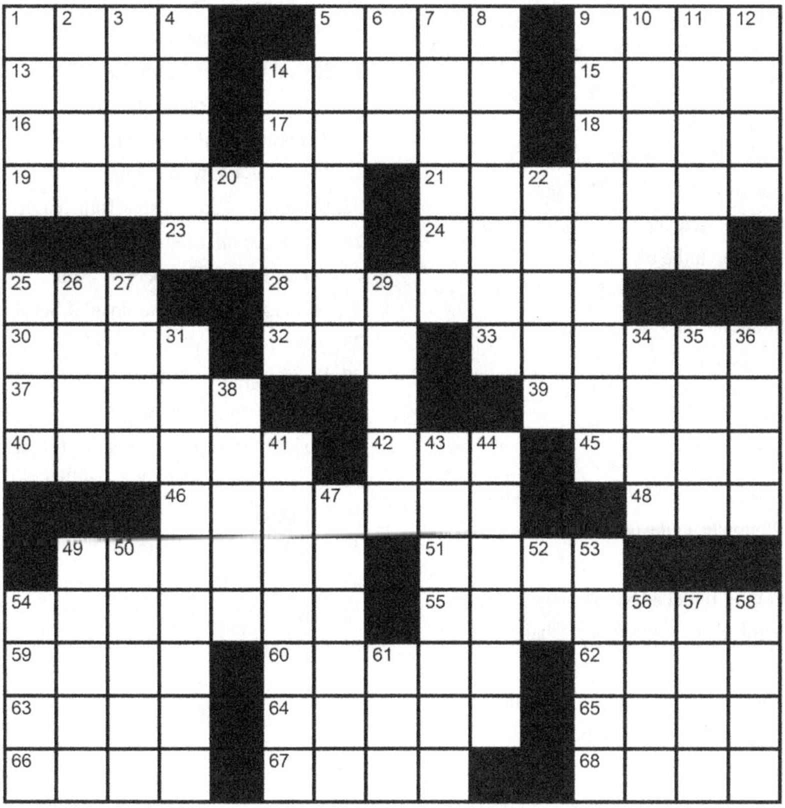

Golf Fact: The average PGA TOUR course is 7000 yards over 18 holes

Across

1. More to tourney lineup
5. Done to bug swarm on course
9. Double birdie AKA
14. Concession food topping
15. Hat sharing risk
16. Pro Robert Cruickshank's middle
17. Birth or coming up of a tourney
19. Golfing, classified as one
20. Steady slow swing is "coveted"
21. PGA Luke Donald's Ill. home (short)
23. Factor of, PGA TOUR vs Champ. TOUR
24. Tiger's father's service
25. Bag, for clubs or gun
27. Caddyshack, Danny's girlfriend
30. South Korean pro NN - Piggy
31. Caddyshack Judge Smails is hit where
32. Course, in the center of
33. Big Daddy Disc Golf
37. Shout during their swing, you are ___
38. 1st, 2nd, or 3rd
39. Under the playing field
40. "50 ft putt" is a tall one
41. Story of Tiger's greatness
42. "Basic Instinct" star & avid golfer
43. Wedge head design
45. Action for course access
46. Poking fun at a friend's swing
49. South Korean pro NN is Chalk Line
50. You're never too.....for golf
51. Thomas Sturges Watson, initially
52. Negative Tiger news, purpose
56. Done to the flag on the green
58. Ones swing every time should be, nearly
60. People say it's amazing, John Daly is ___ alive
61. Walk the hill course, like hiking a mountain
62. Playing mad (slang)
63. Tough, firm grip
64. Swings source of power, from your core
65. High scorer, next hole's tee order

Down

1. Golfers have done it well for years
2. Golf hat protects it (slang)
3. A quality driver really ___ matter to a swing
4. Characteristic "boing" measure of club-face
5. Golf ball pack
6. Direction changing weather to account for
7. Many players colleges group: Abbr
8. Use a wood at this point, likely 1
9. Likelihood to drive the green, pitch-n-putt
10. Hilly Swiss course
11. Round winner's smug manner
12. PGA winning purse size
13. Tournament sign up action & door sign
18. Pattern in old wood club
22. Group of golfers, also a 16th cen. tribe
26. Green fee inflation as of late
27. PGA's front office people: Abbr
28. Ground class - Environmental Sensitive ___
29. Achievement AKA
30. Wise play, ___ golf
32. Friendly golfer are easy to get ___
34. None to open and close on a golf cart (sl)
35. On a golf ball after object collision
36. Dance after a win, like a popular TV show
38. Course designer sketches
42. Collared item bought at pro shop
44. Penick's ___ Red (golf) Book
45. Large grass divots
46. Burnt out club
47. Top-tier pros that tour for $
48. Tourney organizers (short)
49. Pasture course spectator
53. Royal Canadian Golf Assoc.
54. Needed to capture "FORE!" alert
55. The land a course is on
57. Lou G's disease, charity golf tourney: Abbr
59. Nike's ___ fit gear brand

PUZZLE 21

1	2	3	4		5	6	7	8		9	10	11	12	13
14					15					16				
17				18						19				
20							21	22			23			
		24				25			26					
27	28	29				30								
31					32					33	34	35	36	
37				38					39					
40				41				42						
		43	44				45							
46	47	48					49							
50			51			52				53	54	55		
56		57			58	59							
60				61				62					
63				64				65					

Golf Fact: A typical Par-5 hole ranges from between 460-600 yards

Across

1. Beer amounts drank during round
5. Floats on dirty course pond
9. Of ground, flies after contact
13. Plays in Pro-Am
14. Famous Mission Hills locale
15. Mulligan shot
16. "Thread" on shaft, for golf hit drill
17. Par 3 course purpose, before big course
18. National Amputee Golf Assoc.
19. Golf bag holds it (military term)
21. Scorecard has many a ___
23. Fairway marker
24. Sees the course, lie, green etc
25. Golf attire topper
28. Slicer and balls needed per round
30. DeChambeau if Marvel character
32. Mid-range golf disc name
33. Caddyshack judge's name
37. Range btw 16° and 65°
39. 1 bad hole on scorecard
40. Tourney "payment"
42. Long time golfer (short)
45. Surprise reaction to green fee increase
46. Mark, Dean, Oliver & popular clubs
48. Around the Green: Abbr
49. Few pros hold (lit) one to Tiger
51. Ball landing on green, noise
54. Attach items to bag
55. Seasoned, aged, ready to be picked player
59. Ohio Valley Golf Assoc.
60. Even, on leaderboard
62. Slow golf becomes a ___
63. Presidents golf a lot during theirs
64. Daly's dad's job, like Homer's at the power ___
65. Targets: Abbr
66. Eye injury, will likely DNF
67. "Emailed" the membership
68. Disc golf's origin locale (short)

Down

1. Italians bet scores w it
2. Hot & sweaty golf day, effect
3. Golf Shirts
4. Boring TV tourney action, fans fall ___
5. Built course obstruction, artificial
6. Confidence In Action, gear brand
7. Un-seasoned green golfer
8. "Behaviors" of player, hopefully groomed
9. Early/old-time metal driver front
10. Pros still face on TV HUD
11. Second in the Majors won
12. Pro-Am participant. Also, light at night
14. A Golf tourney grouping example
20. Golf stats, numerical (short)
22. Ryder Cup structure
25. Short game shot
26. Hogan's intimidation feel, surrounds
27. Strategy
29. Championship tourney using match play (car)
31. Top identifiable pro golfer has a ___
34. International Assoc. of Golf Admin.
35. The "found it" golfer, usually
36. Southern Nationals Disc Golf
38. Clubs ___ out of bag. Also MLBer into base
41. PGA TOUR, official spelling
43. Signs up to take part in tourney
44. Uncollared clothing OK for Par 3 city course
47. Pay course dues
49. Pros do with the Masters Green Jacket
50. A losing golfer's emotion
52. Honest scores are on the up & ___
53. Mickelson has bet ___
54. Golf camp beds
56. Northern Ohio Golf Assoc.
57. EA Sports stock ticker
58. Sportscaster paper holder
61. Taiwanese PGA pro C.T.

PUZZLE 22

1	2	3	4			5	6	7	8		9	10	11	12
13					14						15			
16					17						18			
19				20			21		22					
		23					24							
25	26	27			28		29							
30			31		32			33			34	35	36	
37				38					39					
40				41		42	43	44		45				
		46			47						48			
	49	50					51		52	53				
54					55				56	57	58			
59				60		61			62					
63				64					65					
66				67					68					

Golf Fact: Trump boasts a 3 HDP

Across

1. Specialist in Education, of golf: Abbr
5. Bay Harbor Golf Club
9. Caddyshack star Chevy
14. Asked "What did you ___ for score?"
15. Pro William Casper's middle
16. Large woods and their weight
17. Methodical player
18. Tourney holders give cheap tix to ___ fans
19. Heated golf rules discussion
20. Accepted excuse for using a power-cart
22. Upper body equipment holder
24. Lessons "bring-up" your game
25. Pro shop 5-finger discount
26. Records are for best ___
27. Outstanding bright as the stars game
32. Grounds crew did for course
34. "The British are coming... to golf" (Benedict)
35. Alt. to sports drink served in course lounge
36. Remembrance golf time (short)
37. Pros NN - Night Fever
41. Pro winner is rewarded on it
44. 67M to 1, same round
46. Idle talk, between shots of course
47. Pro golfer Poulter
48. Easy to get along with golfer
52. Pro golfer Bobby Jones birth town, GA
56. Driving iron AKA
57. Power-cart common color
58. Championship Golf Services Inc
60. When putter is used
61. Nearly 200 US army ___ have courses
62. Player is "happy" to sign card
63. Lob it up and ___ the tree
64. Collection of golfers
65. Southern Nationals Disc Golf
66. Next Tiger / #1 for PGA?

Down

1. Negative news on Tiger, purpose
2. Power-cart plastic kicker
3. Avoid work, play golf
4. Snack cart comes-to-you service
5. Showed up late for golf
6. Power-cart function
7. Course wildlife noise
8. Fingers-crossed it ___ the water
9. Gang of golfers
10. "It's medicinal" smoke during a round (slang)
11. Alumni and Fan Golf Assoc.
12. "Shock" the crowd with hole-in-one
13. Investors "looked at" the course to buy
21. Course wildlife home
23. British Open "rotation" (short)
28. HOF pro Larry Nelson
29. OC at St Andrews #14 known as
30. Eases sunny round burn
31. HOF pro Roberto De Vicenzo
32. Lead hand on top, putt
33. Disc golf discs "dynamic" design
35. Pro salary/win, stat: Abbr
38. HOF pro Tommy Armour
39. Winter golf condition
40. Golf club requires your attire to be
41. Sun seen off course dew
42. Stroke(s) needed, often said as
43. Masters Green Jacket, needs before wearing
45. Food shack offerings
46. Courses at night
49. Fan tribute said to pro. Also a cable channel
50. Not a winner
51. ___ fee for tournament
52. Swedish group, may have watched PGA Europe
53. Ryder Cup grouping
54. LPGA & Euro TOUR player - Hall
55. PGA Champions = ___ 50 and older
59. New "now-type" of player, e.g. Rory

PUZZLE 23

Golf Fact: Biden boasts a 7 HDP

Across

1. Offensive golfer
4. Remembrance golf time (short)
7. The direction of the flag when teeing-off
9. You both cheat, they tell on you = ___ s
10. Golf Tint
12. "Wish" you could be playing golf
13. Pro's NN - The Man w the Plastic Arm
15. Trying the new retail club right there
17. Pro is punished if scorecard isn't
18. Winter golf nose drip
19. Difficulty of a course
21. Hot golf market, continent
22. Caddy can be every round
24. PGA accused of ___ trust
25. Too-tight golf shirt
26. Walk w confidence after big win
28. When practice pays off
30. Even scoring
32. Charged in a cart
35. Good ball flight strategy on Links course
39. Rhode Island Golf Assoc.
40. Leader ranking "drop"
42. Pros and the Green Jacket
44. Nike renowned R&D facility in TX
45. On concession list
46. Caddyshack's Chase as Ty
47. Ball graphic, helps align putt
49. Pro NN - Jacko
52. Tourney field, all of them
53. Course fees for pros, as courtesy
54. HOF Dinah Shore
55. Sportswriter of pro personal lives
56. 1916 PGA Championship win
57. Golf is many athletes "entertainment" (short)
58. Year Round Golf

Down

1. Course varmint
2. Mood of round loser (slang)
3. Course buck
4. Scorecard information
5. Pray to this Norse god for win
6. Assess membership fees
7. Caddyshack's Spaulding, no to golf yes to?
8. Gamblers do w jumbled stats
10. Einstein-ish golfer
11. Snack shack sweet offering
12. Satellite equip to watch tourney
14. LPGA - Walters & Hall
16. Pro travel flight posting: Abbr
17. Shout at in air ball (short)
20. The latest in clubs, like fashion
23. Settles after controversy
27. Hogan's swing was like ___ wine
29. FL / southern course beast (short)
31. Golf TV host's job
32. 2009 Commish. LPGA resigned
33. HOF McCormack, in as non player
34. Arm after a sunny round
36. Intentional curved shot called ___ the ball
37. "Grow" your putting skills
38. Success at mini golf ___ on the angles
39. Tourney no-go zones
41. Lee McLeod Janzen, initially
43. Flag work
48. Fairway worker
50. Shot direction
51. Ball in air, ___ y

PUZZLE 24

Golf Fact: A typical Par-4 hole ranges between 230-460 yards

Across

1. "Own" up to cheating at golf
5. Wet weather condition, still ok to golf
9. Popular 80s sitcom & alien head cover
12. Add, on scorecard
13. Contract upping
14. World Invitational Golf Champ.
16. Warm bit of sunshine
17. Pro-Am participant
18. Pro can ___ you the truth about your swing
19. From winning round celebration cigar
20. Fr. President w 3 HDP
22. Golf Network delay type
23. Course bar gas-filled sign
24. The Open Championship, course style
27. Too far for gimme (slang)
29. An e-cart over night
31. Press called Tiger a ___ been
32. Struggling pro, getting it from the crowd
33. Swing characteristic
36. Play anytime after the sun has
37. Scores put together
39. Snack shack sweet (french)
40. Scorecard render of course/hole layout
41. 18 holes = 18 shots Scotch Whiskey
45. Course discount (short)
46. TOURing players need to know: Abbr
48. Fans, stop and ___ at pros
50. Clean hit w less backspin (slang)
52. Bad round? Remember, it's just ___
53. Course snake's weapon
56. Cart road
57. Golf watching place (old term)
58. Course critters around golfers
59. Fans "stare" at pros
60. Heavy natural object, painted as tee box marker
61. Golf's HOF voting, audio
62. Course buck
63. Tiger's estimated yearly revenue

Down

1. A tourney may have a unique one
2. Ryder Cup '79 added these new players
3. Tall grass hazard
4. Eye injury, will likely DNF the tourney
5. Grand daddy of Majors
6. Start of round w new golf partner (short)
7. Dedication level to favorite course
8. Contract "detail"
9. HOF pro A.W. Tillinghast
10. Club measure from flat surface
11. Fantasy Golf League
12. Actor group, Caddyshack
15. A Golf tourney grouping example
21. Hands on grip
23. Pros asked PGA to "clean-up" the rules
25. Top pros not playing ___ the fans
26. "Eager" to play
28. John Daly's NN
30. Pros are "super" to the avg. golfer
33. Full grouping of golfers
34. Law-troubled Tiger needs one
35. Goosen's demeanor
37. Refill at course lounge
38. Long drive went deep (slang)
39. A lot of talk during round
42. Pro Eduardo Romero's NN
43. SNL alum & "Weeds" star loves golf
44. Daly's spooky on-going battle
47. ___ ist brand
49. Tin Cup, female lead Russo
51. Apple device can play golf video
52. Player's caddy (short)
54. Course menu phrase, fancy
55. " ___ whiz my swing sucks"

PUZZLE 25

Golf Fact: A typical Par-3 hole ranges between 90-230 yards

Across

1. Central Coast Disc Golf
5. Asociación Mexicana Femenil de Golf
9. Eases sunny round burn
10. Major leagues of golf AKA
13. Unwashed sweaty golf attire
14. Standings "jump"
15. Night golf need
16. Post game worn out feeling
17. Flags tourney AKA
19. Tee-time availability request
22. Pro Bobby Locke's first
23. Errors are from "core" game. And tree foot
24. Top golf photographer, Brian
25. Bolt items to bag
26. Double bogeys on fives
27. Martial art cardio in off season
28. First tee, done for picture
30. Fairway woods compared to tee-off wood
33. Right-to-left path AKA
36. Not exact scoring
39. Eat a little at a time of concession offering
42. Defending champs choice, Masters ___
43. Quit the game
45. Club to ball
47. Golf course mighty-planting
48. Player holds out ___ for a win
49. Break-away from the game
51. US Open Qualifying - Local play is
53. Disc golf flick shot
54. 2001 PGA Championship win
55. Mid day round time est.
57. Golf hat, head locale
58. Cart (slang)
59. Press flings at bad player
60. Golf group
61. TOURing players need to know: Abbr
62. Club member's free cart

Down

1. Break in the weather
2. Bunker to bunker, ___ coast
3. Ball in sand, how far
4. International Golf Maintenance
5. Long hitter is, to your team in tourney play
6. Lights up during night golf
7. Very mad at golf score
8. Explosive golfer NN
9. Pro Robert Cruickshank's middle
10. Starters horn
11. Pro golfer Poulter
12. "Scooped" out of trap (slang)
18. HOF artifact add-on
20. Gang of golfers
21. Unkept pond condition
23. Take a drop
27. Phil Mickelson's 1st month
29. Under the fairway sod
31. Phil M, 40k wine, did from Claret jug
32. Barely used course clubs
34. Golf shop item to buy will still have ___
35. Tournament fee
37. Fred Couples birth town, WA
38. Flag removal
40. Play by his own rules, for advantage
41. John Daly vocals, "K.R." album
44. Club from bag, purpose
46. Dangle a tourney invite
48. Club and cleat washing equipment
50. Course operations at night
52. Professional Miniature Golf Assoc.
53. Next-in-line golf partner
56. Missed the tourney cut

PUZZLE 26

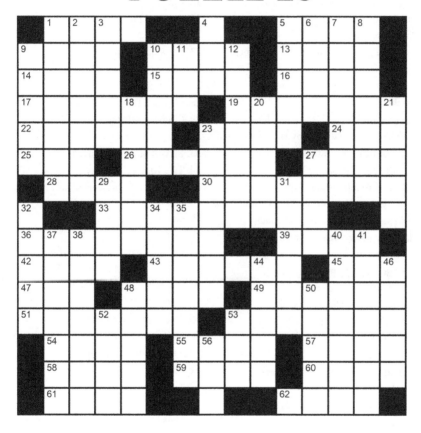

Golf Fact: 85% of the world's countries have golf courses

Across

1. Scott Macpherson Golf Design
5. Jacksonville Area Golf Assoc.
9. American Soc. of Golf Course Arch.
14. Clubhouse entrance
15. Some players indulge in this green (slang)
16. Keeps your clubs in the cart
17. Targeted by early disc golfer
18. Pros risk penalty unless scorecard is ___
19. Talk between rival pros
20. Mickelson odyssey putter
22. Long putter removes hand ___ movement
24. Pro Paul Runyan's middle
26. Famous actor Dennis, loves golf
27. Pro shop buy-all
30. Long putter, swings ___ a pendulum
31. 2019 Documentary VO'd by Bill Murray
32. Neat and tidy golf shirts tend to be
36. Majority of golf champs locale
37. Pro travel flight posting: Abbr
38. SEGA videogame console w golf game (90s)
43. Nicklaus NN, often without "golden"
47. Masters winner "wears" Green Jacket
48. Team vs team
49. Make sense of, or play out the rules
52. Golf shoe lace bunching
53. Choosing moderate priced clubs
55. Golf cart going uphill
59. Happy Gilmore
60. "Mix" of reactions from Tiger gossip
62. International Golf Society of Taipei
63. Unable to sum a scorecard
64. Player's awful showing and 70's game show
65. Old Ladies Golf Assoc.
66. 1936 PGA Championship win, Shute
67. "Spot" on hole
68. Golf HOF to St. Augustine

Down

1. Golf Channel broadcast feed to old TVs
2. Course prices "increased"
3. Power-cart motor
4. Look good for game, and a kid-show Mr.
5. HOF pro John Henry Taylor
6. Course maintenance
7. Exhale noise on ball strike
8. Needed after long tiring game
9. Lost ball penalty
10. Golf pant pattern and range-ball markings
11. Hold club in hand, and rhymes with clasp
12. Class of golfers
13. Average Putts per Hole, stat
21. 140-180 ___ s is a typical 18-hole course
23. Carts quiet engines
25. Oregon Golf Review
27. Punch the ball
28. First tee, for picture with group
29. Course mortgage
30. Long Putters
33. Play of pro was "noticed"
34. TOURing players need to know: Abbr
35. Carts ___ around course fast, & pub game obj.
39. Golf digest number
40. "Association" of golfers
41. Unlucky ball lands then rolls ___ hazard
42. Sunrise, Sunset tee-times: Abbr
43. Arm after a sunny round
44. Houston Golf Assoc.
45. Keep open for a FORE!
46. Golf industry pulls in 70 ___ annually
50. Clubs rubber-grips, over time
51. Tin Cup cameo, pro Corey
52. Southern course beast (short)
54. Nebraska Senior Golf Assoc.
56. Fans "stare" at or "eyeball" the pros
57. Wyoming State Golf Assoc.
58. Tiger, Rory, or DJ....of the golf world
59. Season turning point
61. Richmond Golf Assoc.

PUZZLE 27

1	2	3	4		5	6	7	8		9	10	11	12	13
14					15					16				
17					18					19				
20				21		22			23					
			24		25				26					
27	28	29						30						
31								32				33	34	35
36												37		
38			39	40	41	42		43	44	45	46			
			47					48						
49	50	51					52							
	53				54				55		56	57	58	
59					60			61		62				
63					64					65				
66					67					68				

Golf Fact: Florida is the state with the most courses, 1000+

Across

1. Pros do w The Green Jacket
6. 9 down, and 9 ___
10. American Seniors Golf Association
14. Praise is, onto pros
15. World Wide Golf Club
16. PGA Championship
17. Florida course reptiles (short)
18. Tee box hits per hole
19. Shop for cheap used clubs
20. Tee box markers "make" border
22. Golf course, federal regulation area
24. Diez grande, Spanish tour prize $
26. Golf videogame on this Panasonic console (90s)
29. Carts have just fwd and rev
34. Tour's "geographical" territory (short)
35. Tourney details (slang)
38. Masters Jacket ceremony takes place in Butler ___ most years
39. Hotel to course movers
41. Light rain ___, keep playing
43. Course walker's muscles have it
44. Rumors do to Tiger's overall rep
46. Tourney watcher are assigned them
48. Ryder Cup PGA participant
49. Turf type for hitting balls
50. Tiger's rep as of late
52. Between Pitch and Sand
56. So-so golfer
60. Food shack offerings
64. Strange brew, course lounge
65. Tiger Woods mother (short)
67. "Redeem" your scoring prowess
68. Rare results across four-somes
69. Ottawa Disc Golf Club
70. Driving range enclosure
71. Practice swing
72. Stinky old golf shoes
73. Pro NN - Answer Man

Down

1. Arnold Palmer Course Designer
2. Your straights when losing badly
3. Pro Henrik Stenson's middle
4. Golf TV host's job
5. Has the NN - Answer Man
6. Golf team minimum
7. PGA to the Golf HOF
8. Georgia Golf Course Super. Assoc.
9. Pebble Beach famous 18th, to the left
10. A course reservation is essentially this: Abbr
11. Seniors' Golf Assoc. of Arkansas
12. Fans stop and ___ at god-like pro
13. Junior golfer problem
21. Tourney has completed
23. Savannah Disc Golf Club
25. Fans going to live games
26. Tenn. Golf Course Superintendent. Assoc.
27. "Piles" of balls lost in the pond
28. Caddyshack's gopher puppet
30. Do it at the snack shack
31. Jerky club, ball can go just ___ anywhere
32. Ball washer will scrub and ___ your ball
33. PGA TOUR pro with the most titles
36. Cheaters free-stroke club
37. "String" of tourney wins
40. Knighted Faldo has this honor
42. Craig Stadler's NN
45. Nike golf, swoosh
47. Flag color and placement
51. PGA has been asked to "clean-up" the rules
53. Half of pro-am pair, possibility
54. Ryder Cup reward
55. Approach worker
56. Mario Golf Toadstool Tour videogame
57. Northern Ohio course water neighbor
58. A quality driver really ___ matter
59. International Golf Society of Taipei
61. Golf Magazine ___ r
62. Golf sock may go all the way to it
63. Grass crew maintenance supply
66. A duffer's cry

PUZZLE 28

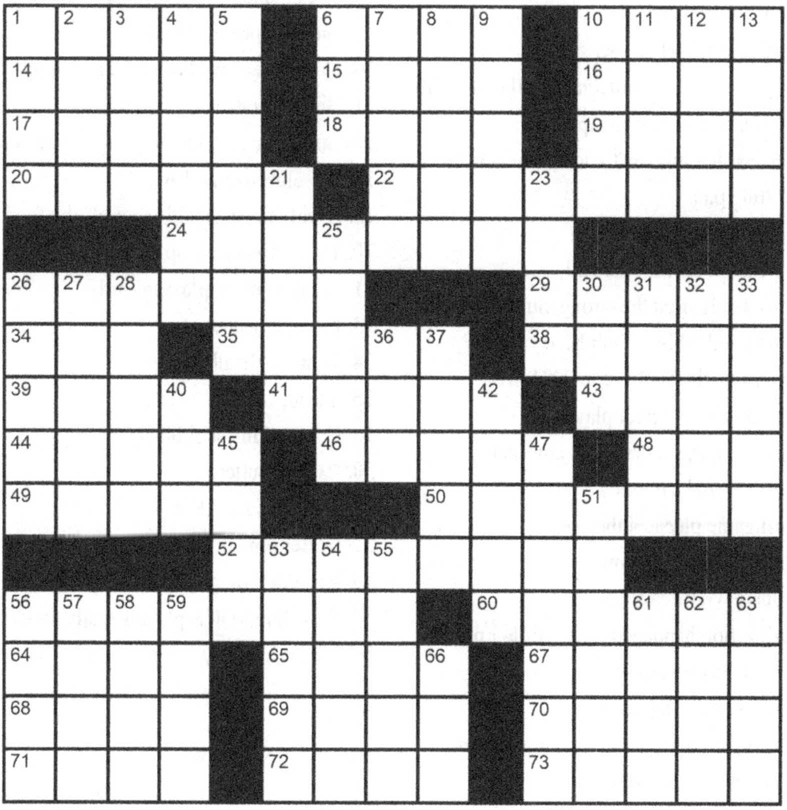

Golf Fact: Portland OR, has 4.48 courses per 100,000 residents

Across

1. Dorf on Golf, character's 1st name
5. Players want "a way in" to HOF
11. Driving range enclosure
12. Tiger's rep as of late
14. Tee box markers "make" border
15. OC at St Andrews #3
16. Punch the ball
17. US Open's youngest ever, 14yr old Zhang
18. Top Ten Finishes, stat
19. Anthracite Golf Assoc.
20. Course corporate structure, legal entity: Abbr
21. The Open Championship month
22. Players that just can't win are in them
24. Golfing pair
25. Post game beat-up feeling
26. Line them up with the ball
27. Mistakenly used the wrong club: Abbr
28. Mud piled all over club head
29. PGA TOUR Par 4 ace in 2001, M___
31. Pro D.J. is ___ great player
32. Pros walk the course with confidence
34. Score to make tourney cut (short)
35. Post game physical therapy
39. Processes large quantities of golf equipment
40. Course wildlife offense
41. Ball action happened after a little English
42. Hard to watch injury
43. Early season skin tone
44. Tickets to tourneys ___ getting expensive
45. "Let 'er ___ " (hit slang)
46. Need help with your game? ___ a pro
47. Tiger soaked up everything as a young golfer
50. Golf clubs are made from various "metals"
52. Hit next shot from where ball ___
53. 3rd party will define ruling
54. Tourney will "happen" this weekend
55. 1774 1st champ, Rattray. His job
56. Cart in reverse

Down

1. Lessons will ___ your ballooning score
2. Closing a golf course in summer is pure ___
3. Course redo (short)
4. Pro must win occasionally to ___ pro card
5. Golf Channel's Uverse partner
6. Jokers Wild tourney uses playing ___
7. Muni course locale
8. PGA broadcast language (short)
9. A golfer's physical make-up
10. Green fees have been paid and approved
11. Golf videogamers' organization
13. Going-for-it and hoping to ___ the odds
14. SW club size vs driver
15. Event at course will "supply" the food
20. Tourney sells cheap tix to ___ fans
21. Tourney using playing cards - ___ Wild
23. Lit night game sky
24. Tourney detail (slang)
25. Snead, "Play it Again, ___ "
28. Cart parking stall blocker
30. "Belly" putter
31. Course place AKA
32. Golfer rep after rumors spread
33. Ball cut through the water like one
34. Traveling TOUR players really rack'em up
36. Scores honestly, on the ___ (3wd)
37. 1st USA 400+ yd Long Drive Champ, Clayton
38. Pro's NN - Answer Man
40. Course fees waved in exchange for a favor
42. Pro Marlene Hagge's NN
43. Towel, ___ bag .....like donkey tail
46. Feel it more in summer rounds
47. Wrinkled golf shirt makes you look like one
48. Game's speed of play, kept up by marshal
49. Tee box hit per hole
51. Pros may wear for TV tourney

PUZZLE 29

Golf Fact: Over 456 million rounds of golf are played annually, worldwide

Across

1. Helps power shots
5. Arnold Palmer Course Designer
9. Done during speed golf
13. Fix-up clubhouse (slang)
14. Fade or hook
15. International Golf Psychology Assoc.
16. Fans fawn & ___ over the Pros
17. First golf videogame 1978, ___ vox
18. You birdie and leader bogeys =
19. Pro and notable Callaway user Henrik
21. Pro's autograph action
23. "How many shots did you ___ on #8?"
24. Streaming tours seen here
25. William Ben Hogan, initially
28. "Dangle" a sweet tourney invite
30. Using 6 instead of 9
32. HOF golfer and Pres. Dwight D. Eisenhower
33. DNF, with ___
37. Luxury box hors d'oeuvres offering
39. Club grips over time
40. Caddyshack's Judge Smails soda of choice
42. PGA a-ok w this nature friendly gov't body
45. These Indian inspired stretches may improve your golf game
46. From wearing cap all day
48. LPGA golfer Lottie D.
49. If you jerk club = shoulders ___ engage
51. North Dakota Golf Assoc.
54. Pro Bob Estes's NN
55. Driving range's peak level
59. Range btw 16° and 65°
60. Greenside rough
62. Walk & swing means you are cap___ of golfing
63. Lucky bounce can do it for bad shot
64. Budget clubs may "emulate" top brand
65. Back feeling from over-twisting taking shot
66. Investors "looked-at" the course to buy
67. Course critters, for the most part
68. Sportswriter folly

Down

1. More players to tourney lineup
2. Errors are from "core" game. Also, the underground of a tree
3. Watcher does to tourney commercials
4. Post game worn out feeling
5. Tiger's dominance in 2021 (3wd)
6. Tee AKA
7. PGA tells media not to report results
8. Sink(ed) putt (slang)
9. HOF decider, golf celeb
10. 2021 -Will Tiger play ever ___?
11. Flexes during swing
12. Tourney plaques, on wall
14. Bested badly (slang) & did w victory cigar
20. Scoring Average, stat
22. Sunglasses ease it during round
25. World Golf Teachers Federation
26. CAN Weir's Masters Dinner menu
27. Player, for a win. Also, Obama's ___ & Change
29. Event Tent at First Nations course
31. Wearing slick, up-to-date golf clothes
34. Original golf balls, like original clubs
35. Atlanta Disc Golf Organization
36. Low score
38. Golf hat protects it from sunburn
41. $ tours ___ the best pros
43. Masters Jacket 'green' is ___ 342
44. Accidental ball tap, stroke penalty
47. "Excitement" and mania of The Masters
49. A first try at golf
50. Backswinged club to golfer's head
52. HOF pro Gary Player
53. Players must "conform" to the new PGA rules
54. Links green undulation
56. Club bidding site
57. Short online video
58. Numbers game sports betters play
61. Range of Motion

PUZZLE 30

1	2	3	4		5	6	7	8		9	10	11	12
13					14					15			
16					17					18			
19				20			21		22				
		23				24							
25	26	27			28		29						
30			31		32				33			34	35	36
37				38						39				
40					41		42	43	44		45			
		46			47							48		
	49	50						51		52	53		
54							55				56	57	58
59					60		61				62		
63					64						65		
66					67						68		

Golf Fact: 78% of golfers are male, 22% are female

Across

1. PGA accused of ___ trust
5. Vice Golf ball line
9. On air golf
14. A single w a 3-some
15. Rhode Island Golf Assoc.
16. Caddyshack's Murray's no-prep char.
17. Course rating
19. Horizontal swing ___
20. A tee time must do on sunny days
21. Course navigation
23. Pro store, ___ chandise
24. Pre round prayer, ending
25. Caddyshack amongst golf movies
27. Club usage decision
30. Money for course access
31. Lay-up shot, to trouble
32. Should direct a golf movie
33. National Amputee Golf Assoc.
37. Holston Hills, Knoxville locale (short)
38. Seeded fairway grass
39. Walks through green lies
40. Golf course obstacle
41. Kick wedge contact
42. Large club selection
43. Range place
45. Wet Winter golf condition
46. Fee for tournament
49. Blindside
50. Arnold Daniel Palmer initially
51. Press ques. needs ans ___
52. Golf shirts tend to be
56. Lay-up, short of what shot ___ reach
58. Rare GUR stake
60. X-out ball meaning
61. Hogan's intimidation feel
62. Alumni and Fan Golf Assoc.
63. 1936 PGA Championship win, Shute
64. Golf Guide to Mexico
65. Golf attire

Down

1. Knocked out ball
2. Course open during winter?
3. Study pros for
4. Prepped to play golf
5. Big hitter
6. Play when the sun has
7. Indiana Golf Assoc.
8. Caddyshack true FL course had none
9. Course membership #s
10. Arthur D'Arcy "Bobby" Locke initially
11. My clubs are at fault
12. Caddyshack's dialogue exchange
13. Gave Caddyshack 2.5/4
18. Guns-a-blazing golf
22. Caddy provides helping one
26. 19 PGA TOUR wins, B.C.
27. 180 to 500, electric cart
28. Up and ___ hazard
29. 1918 PGA Championship winner
30. Essential item hanging from bag
32. Portable beer storage
34. Eases sun burn
35. Seen on pasture quality course
36. Address the ball (short)
38. Pro winner is rewarded here
42. Tee box to hit from, for a challenge
44. Not-so-good golfer
45. Watch tours live online
46. Staggered tee-times
47. Do w The Green Jacket
48. Autograph, not happening
49. 90's was a growth ___ for golf
53. Flag in hole = ___ to hit
54. Edmonton Disc Golf Assoc.
55. "___ Golf", pros famous love-letter 2020
57. UK course location (short)
59. Carry huge bag

PUZZLE 31

1	2	3	4		5	6	7	8		9	10	11	12	13
14					15					16				
17				18						19				
20							21	22			23			
		24					25			26				
27	28	29				30								
31					32					33	34	35	36	
37				38						39				
40				41				42						
		43	44				45							
46	47	48				49								
50				51			52			53	54	55	
56			57		58	59							
60				61					62				
63				64					65				

Golf Fact: 54 is the average age of golfers in the U.S.

Across

1. Golfer movers
5. Solid piece of mud on clubhead
9. Negative older female golfers
13. Pros are not given tourney spot, must ___ it
14. Scorecard uses thick, heavy weight
15. Mood of round loser (slang)
16. Seniors' Golf Assoc. of Arkansas
17. Buy Calloway, TaylorMade or
18. Back may experience after twisting swing
19. Heckler attempts to on a swinger
21. Breath catching after walking hilly course
23. Watch golf in "man-cave / hideaway"
24. They lift flagstick while you putt
25. Swiss mountain golf
28. Golf in a "threesome"
30. Heavy laugh after golf joke
32. College player's E-address ending
33. Let them win, for business sake
37. Common course flyer
39. Sign - "No spikes upon ___ "
40. Fr. pro Jug McSpaden first
42. Steven Charles Stricker, initially
45. Fans go, over fav. pro. Also famous singer
46. Course wildlife, from bushes
48. Loses all golf wagers, believes all golf stories
49. Golf balls packaging, likely 3
51. Golfer's big gut, when bent forward
54. Hit ball into water, then make par (slang)
55. Golf glove, strap action
59. More than 1 even hole
60. Leads up to green
62. Infected injury does this
63. Modred Mallet Putter maker ___lf
64. Ryder Cup structure
65. Three Rivers Golf Association
66. Young golfer
67. PGA TOUR game - EA Sports stock ticker
68. Nose drips it during winter golf

Down

1. Winner vs loser score
2. European Amateur Golf Tour
3. Golf Range Assoc. of America
4. Golf shoe lace kerfuffle
5. Clubhouse rented room chow
6. Average Putts per Hole
7. 2011 PGA Championship win, Bradley
8. All over the place golfer
9. Golf "event"
10. 2021 -Will Tiger play ever ___?
11. "Dull repetition" of golf practice
12. "Best Colonel Bogey"
14. Mannerly golfer
20. HOF Tommy Armour
22. Hot-wired a cart, drove away
25. Maintain it in back, swing
26. Italians bet scores w it
27. No money to golf
29. Tin Cup, female lead Rene
31. Chapman system team format
34. TOURing players need to know: Abbr
35. New England Golf Assoc.
36. Golf course obstacle
38. Weather resistant shirt, feel
41. Play different today
43. Pre hit warmup, rituals
44. Golf glove permanence
47. "Stick around" clubs
49. Golf cart co-op
50. Membership fee size for most
52. Golf Gallery
53. Golf is all about long and short ones
54. Garcia, 2007 CA Championship, did in cup
56. Pro w multiple sponsor offers
57. Popular power cart brand
58. Club requires your golf attire to be
61. Tells everyone about your cheating

PUZZLE 32

Golf Fact: The average golf handicap is between 13 and 15

Across

1. Winners can do it after win, but shouldn't
5. Different Strokes Golf Assoc.
9. Quick swing
14. Golf particular
15. Non combustion carts (short)
16. Double birdie AKA
17. Tiger rumors, often ___ ymous
18. "I never cheat" golfer
19. Play anytime after the sun has
20. Course walkers
22. Golfer's left out
24. To put names on golf trophy
25. NN - Supermodel of the Fairways (S. Korean)
26. Hole-in-one, past
27. Tiger's talk-trouble, in childhood
32. Tee box marker distinction
34. "I 'guess' we can hit"
35. Below Average Golfer
36. "Let 'er ___" (hit - slang)
37. Course crew for grounds
41. Wedge head design
44. Drive time club
46. Ball damage possibility if hit rock
47. PGA's - Chief Operating Officer: Abbr
48. Young golfers wear clothing w it
52. Garage wall air caddy
56. Driving iron AKA
57. Half of pro-am pair, possibility
58. Club transfer, temporary
60. 18th hole
61. Wise play from wise golfer
62. Tee box boundary
63. Lob the ball up and ___ the hazard
64. Pros Crocker & O'Hair
65. Fan going to live game
66. Mini golf.... ___ on the angles

Down

1. Push cart safety tech.
2. Tiger's had a ___ w the law
3. Drive ___ the cart path, say the rules
4. Municipal course - Open to the ___ public
5. Amazon will ___ golfballs directly to you
6. Golf shots & most bread
7. Golf Equipment Aficionados
8. Knock-down shot, vs wind
9. Winners play the game dead ___
10. You will, on slow paced course
11. International Golf Society of Taipei
12. "Escape" work, go golfing
13. Done to the pin / flag, when others are putting
21. South of border tourney food possibility
23. Golf data type
28. Tournament Series
29. After 9th
30. Crowd does with noise
31. Practice Repetition i.e. swings (short)
32. "Las Vegas" star & avid golfer
33. Mastergrip line of putters
35. Bing Crosby Open
38. HOF Ian Woosnam
39. Club help situation, likely, at par 3 course
40. Golf course enforcer e.g. marshal
41. Negative news on Tiger
42. "Perfect shot, straight down the ___"
43. Masters Green Jacket needs before wearing
45. L or R bend in fairway
46. Absorb golf lessons like a ___
49. To want the latest in club trend, greatly
50. Connects shaft to clubhead
51. Fee type to get into tournament
52. Course lake resident
53. Bugs Bunny's round sponsor
54. Golf Tourney Assoc. of America
55. Animal or brass instrument tourney starter
59. Old Tokyo Tourney, locale

PUZZLE 33

1	2	3	4		5	6	7	8		9	10	11	12	13
14					15					16				
17					18					19				
20			21			22	23						
24						25							
		26				27			28	29	30	31
	32	33					34						
35										36			
37			38	39	40			41	42	43			
44					45		46						
			47				48				49	50	51
52	53	54	55				56						
57					58	59				60			
61					62					63			
64					65					66			

Golf Fact: $70 Billion - the worth of the golf industry, annually

Across

1. Range of Motion
4. Players medical pros (short)
7. Golf videogame on Google streaming service
9. "Hit" the ball, like it deserved it
10. HOF pro Doug Ford
12. Famous swing coach, Butch
13. Fills out scorecard
15. When the Masters is played
17. Change one thing in swing
18. North Dakota Golf Assoc.
19. Burn Center Golf Invitational
21. PGA TOUR Champions, ___ 50 and older
22. 3 golfers
24. Horn noise to start the tourney
25. Fans express surprise about scandal
26. Ball dimples ___ wind resistance
28. Driving range lesson is schooling for golf ___
30. Copy scores on new scorecard
32. Thick rough (slang)
35. Mini golf nearly gone at the ___ the 1930s
39. Reaction from Tiger gossip is a "mix"
40. Kick-wedge action
42. Slow start to tourney
44. ___ out of the way of golfer teeing-off
45. Golfing while carrying ___ s 300-400 cal. /h
46. "Prohibit" a vote for new PGA commish,
47. Ground ball keeps going
49. Team versus another
52. Course shop
53. Pro Peter Oosterhuis NN
54. Tournament Director
55. Range catchers
56. This team "will go against" that team
57. Vegas gambling O ___

Down

1. Overgrown Links grass
2. Hot & sweaty golf day, result from player
3. Size of cart tires
4. Course at night
5. Speed battle for top spot
6. Pack away your clubs, likely in this closet
7. 5x Long Drive Champ Carlborg
8. A deplorable 10-hole score to overall score
10. Caddyshack II reception (very negative)
11. Unspoiled golfer
12. Golf crossword phrase
14. Tease friend about their tatter-like swing
16. Lee Buck Trevino, initially
17. "___ birdie!" (possessive)
20. "Jan, jerking the club ___ power and the prize"
23. Pros aren't given it, they must ___ their spot in the tourney
27. Missing safety in a golf cart
29. Ball mark after collision with rock
31. Ball scrub-washer action
32. Why clubs are in the garage
33. Turn body on backswing
34. Rory McIlroy nationality, N.
36. Plan "maker", or coach came up w strategy
37. Course must be ___ golf, the lights are on
38. Flag pole to cup
39. Wise play
41. Talent is in the pro's "genes"
43. Fans ___ over a pro golfer
48. Dishonest golfer, many times
50. "I can't play so Jim will ___ the group's 4th"
51. Pro's NN - The Tower

58. Golf's Faldo knighted as one

70

PUZZLE 34

Golf Fact: 2 million - the number of people employed in the golfing industry worldwide

Across

1. Pro Julius Boros NN
5. Tourney medical is under one
9. Player's health advisors: Abbr
12. Victory puff from this
13. Water shade on golf shirt
14. Group of golfers (animal ref)
16. Fore!
17. Golf cart tire bulge
18. Contract upping
19. Course redos
20. Make up rumor about golfer, legally ___
22. A teammate quickly becomes one
23. Picked and ready to golf
24. Pros do with The Green Jacket
27. Pro shop visit, purpose
29. Walking the course, fitness "routine"
31. Bounces on links green
32. Caddy may ___ a strategy
33. LPGA golfer Dinah
36. Tiger, huge man in the golf world
37. Plays by his own rules
39. Indoor putting done in a room like this
40. PGA TV slot
41. Mini golf is all about the
45. Tourney staff may ___ a "Quiet" sign
46. Golf pun
48. Don't drive a power-cart ___ the green
50. Pro Scott Simpson's NN
52. Pro's NN - Bantam Ben
53. Collegiate golf body
56. Course field vs range matt
57. Golfers will "come together" as a team
58. Game of Golf Institute
59. Ohio Valley Golf Assoc.
60. Front and back halves of course
61. PGA Europe terr. (short)
62. Young golfer
63. Ball lifters

Down

1. Multi-cart collision
2. PGA TOUR season program
3. Funny imitation of favorite golfer
4. PGA TOUR game maker Electronic ___
5. Score added
6. Golf supplies (short)
7. Club range ID system
8. Network delay type
9. Player, triumphant saying
10. Jack & Jill golfers = ___ & ___
11. Golf legends in paint
12. Player's food energy source (short)
15. Satisfactory golf balls & tees
21. Bad streaming of golf tourney
23. Course fee coupon action
25. Diplomatic & International Golf Assoc.
26. Lie is the ball at ___
28. Mass made club manufacturing became more prevalent starting in 19 ___
30. Pro Lloyd Mangrum's middle
33. Greatest Game Ever Played, star LaBeouf
34. HOF exhibit, popular content displayed
35. Course breakfast, for golfers and a horse
37. Course crew for grounds
38. Take ball out of hazard
39. 10,000 golf hours
42. Canadian $, ball marker
43. A cart go'er
44. United PGA place
47. Pro's face on TV HUD
49. Aces
51. Horse-like paced play
52. So-so pro is still in the playoff ___
54. Pro in the PGA wheel
55. Ball carry is a ball in the what?

PUZZLE 35

Golf Fact: Callaway makes $1 Billion+ in revenue each year

Across

1. Alumni and Fan Golf Assoc.
5. 140-180 ___ s make up typical 18-hole
9. PGA Commish (slang)
10. PGA TOUR Champions = ___ 50 and older
13. Quirky director should direct a golf movie
14. Cart path
15. Truck type transports GolfTV equip.
16. After Work Golf Cup
17. Long Drive Champ Zuback's HOF home
19. Ball rockets off club like a
22. Power-carts are typically a two -___
23. Asked of a ball in flight
24. When pro tour plays rained-out round (short)
25. Press called Tiger an old ___ been
26. Ironically putting machine's have
27. Lie is the ball at ___
28. Cushion in golf cart
30. Course trees act as, to noise
33. Pro's NN - Tutta
36. Mini golf 18th, ball capture method
39. Deep grass divot (slang)
42. Temporary club possession
43. Forced carry obstacle
45. Gets you a "thank you" by course staff
47. Mickelson's wife
48. ___, when the pro is speaking
49. LPGA's first event location outside USA
51. Lumpy, unkept course hole
53. Golf time-share meeting
54. Golfer critique (slang)
55. Nebraska Senior Golf Assoc.
57. Ball mark from hitting e.g. rock
58. Crowd does with noise
59. Too-tight golf shirt
60. Major injuries, rush to emerg ___
61. Golfer movers
62. Golf game "type"

Down

1. Bloomers at the Masters
2. Rare winner, John Daly's sponsor appeal
3. Pre round handshake
4. Pro William Earl Mehlhorn, initially
5. Having ___ of the yips
6. Used for golf gloves
7. Walking the course, fitness "process"
8. Wrap hands on grip
9. Clubs connect, like un-matching swords
10. Turf type for hitting balls
11. Golf Equipment Aficionados
12. Pitch n putt hole and Par 3 hole
18. Temporary clubs that get around
20. On concession list
21. Fee for tournament and door to club
23. Score of 10 on hole (slang)
27. Course redo (short)
29. A reservation is a player-to-course: Abbr
31. 1923 PGA Championship course
32. Keeps your clubs in the cart
34. Course measurement, all yards
35. Overflow of golf balls and tees
37. Club house design redo
38. Legal to declare ball unplayable
40. Tiger's dominance, today (3wd)
41. Golf membership payment option
44. Every golfer does it when nobody's looking
46. After golf celebration
48. In TV broadcast booth
50. Captures the pro tourney
52. Health and Safety In Golf
53. Scottish Golf Union
56. Did in power cart

PUZZLE 36

Golf Fact: Men drive an average of 226 yards, woman drive an average of 148 yards

Across

1. Most glove the left
5. Inter. Golf Society of Taipei
9. Clubs take up, in trunk
14. PGA TOUR Par 4 ace in 2001, M___
15. Golf bag purpose, & wheat storage
16. Perfect hit is as straight as this
17. "Flip" through golf catalogue
18. GolfTown warehouse store, equip. available
19. Event location
20. Pro NN - Robopro
22. Enclosed driving range
24. Check opponents bag for club use, legally
26. Jordan, winner of 2015 U.S. Open
27. "Smear" media coverage of tourney
30. PGA Championship
31. Golf, became ___ more popular in 2000s
32. Pay for power
36. Seen on skirted female golfer
37. Backswing flaw fix = you must ___ off the club
38. Legal to putt with
43. Rare winner, John Daly's sponsor appeal
47. Big guy on team
48. Mini golf in early 20th C.
49. Leave the golf course, empty
52. Par 3 drive, ___ land on the green
53. Pro "image" on tourney media
55. Store your clubs out of sight
59. Angered golfer. Also, self reviewing a course
60. Pro NN - Radar
62. Stash golf bag away. Also, animal skin
63. Came up short
64. Bag carrier (slang)
65. European Disabled Golf Assoc.
66. Door to clubhouse
67. Equip. info or stat (short)
68. Study clubs

Down

1. Golfing keeps you ___ & hearty
2. PGA TOR Champions - ___ 50 and older
3. Clubs require golfer's attire to be
4. "1-Piece Takeaway" for jerking club
5. Watch TOUR from this space: Abbr
6. Pro Henry Picard's middle
7. Weather resist shirt, feel
8. Dwelling seen from St. Andrews in Scotland
9. Narrowly avoid a bogey
10. I see my shot kicking right
11. Legend Arnold Palmer NN
12. Done after every shot and hole
13. Head cover material supplier
21. Old pro Ballesteros' last
23. Carolina Senior Golf Assoc.
25. Your place when front-9 becomes a memory
27. Professional Miniature Golf Assoc.
28. Course mortgage
29. Ben Hogan's service
30. Golf videogame Windows machine (short)
33. Flapper
34. Swing with it = best chance at success
35. Investors ___ the course to buy after looking at everything worth seeing
39. Tee time reservation, a form of
40. Same odds as becoming pro
41. Bought a club and played a round with it
42. Ball Striking, stat
43. Rich course growth
44. Olson of LPGA
45. Range catchers
46. Vijay Singh's family member, also pro
50. Greenside rough, and kitchen garb
51. PGA Tour's "West ___ Swing"
52. Attach bag to cart with rope, string or other
54. Helps power shots
56. Poor course revenue, may need
57. South Dakota Golf Assoc.
58. Where the Club's weight is
59. Ball in the air is a project ___
61. Winter golf time (short)

PUZZLE 37

1	2	3	4		5	6	7	8		9	10	11	12	13
14					15					16				
17					18					19				
20				21		22			23					
			24		25				26					
27	28	29					30							
31							32				33	34	35	
36											37			
38			39	40	41	42		43	44	45	46			
		47					48							
49	50	51				52								
	53				54				55		56	57	58	
59				60			61		62					
63				64					65					
66				67					68					

Golf Fact: 14 clubs max, are allowed in a PGA TOUR competitor's bag

Across

1. Starters horn
6. Wayne County Men's Am. champ.
10. "All" leather gloves
14. Pros getting PGA qualifying run-around become
15. Pros joke that legend Ben Hogan ___ green
16. Methodical player
17. Collection of golfers
18. Super golfer sinks winning putt for team
19. 2 tourneys on TV, take your ___
20. Daly's on-going battles
22. Golf TV comes to you over them
24. Pro tour event is "told"
26. Plays for fun, not for $
29. Golf equipment AKA
34. Clubhead slow down, Also streaming buffer
35. Golf lesson AKA
38. Pro Ricky Fowler's clubs
39. Aces
41. Game wager preferred payment
43. Not seen on golfer because of hat
44. Quadruple bogeys on fives
46. PGA TOUR vs all other Tours
48. Course Manager: Abbr
49. Old moth ___ golf clothes
50. Course bin holds what?
52. Negative Tiger news, purpose
56. Old Course at St Andrews #3
60. "Excitement" of the tourney, Also alcohol
64. Many a ___ walked golfing
65. Ball from bag, action
67. Air audio problem, during Caddyshack filming
68. Darling Downs Golf Association
69. Records TV golf, old tech
70. Best pros
71. Bags on cart
72. Major U.S. Championship every year in June
73. Pro's bobble heads

Down

1. Bryson James Aldrich DeChambeau, initially
2. Golf's w a limp
3. Happy Gilmore actor, Sandler
4. Stay and golf here
5. Has the NN - Answer Man
6. William Ben Hogan, initially
7. Free and ___ of hazard
8. Golfer deserved it based on virtue and ___
9. Pros love and ___ The Green Jacket
10. Pro golfer Julius Boros's NN
11. Many golfers go here prior to turning pro (short)
12. Running Battle for top spot
13. Woodland course wildlife. Add an "S"
21. Autograph, not happening
23. Walton Disc Golf Club
25. Caddyshack 'constellation' Production Co.
26. Playing without friends
27. Media "craziness" surrounded Tiger for years
28. HOF member McCormack, non-player
30. Tourney fan mild wonder reaction
31. Presidential golf no show
32. Device to hang things off bag
33. Pro Walt Burkemo's NN
36. Lodewicus Theo "Louis" Oosthuizen, initially
37. Club flies out of hands, reason
40. "Observe" course layout
42. Pros Crocker & O'Hair
45. Southern Nationals Disc Golf
47. New ball must be, after lost ball
51. Pro Bob Tway's NN
53. Intern. Assoc. of Golf Travel Operations
54. Hitting ___ AKA indoor golf mat
55. Bad reaction to snack shack
56. Team coach, militarily (short)
57. Poor course revenue, owners may need
58. Raveneaux Ladies Golf Assoc.
59. Old gloves show wear and ___
61. Part of OOB fencing
62. PGA TOUR outside US (short)
63. Golf ball props
66. Positive, sweet cheer from French crowd

PUZZLE 38

1	2	3	4	5		6	7	8	9		10	11	12	13
14						15					16			
17						18					19			
20				21		22			23					
		24			25									
26	27	28							29	30	31	32	33
34				35		36	37		38				
39			40		41			42		43			
44			45		46				47		48		
49						50		51					
			52	53	54	55							
56	57	58	59					60		61	62	63	
64				65		66		67					
68				69			70						
71				72			73						

Golf Fact: 41% of a round's shots come from a putter

Across

1. Test wind, grass action
5. Sketch of hole on the scorecard
11. Municipal course yearly fee
12. Bags & drinks holders located here (3wd)
14. Cart ID number
15. Go-for-it attitude
16. Dangled trophy to golfer like this to a donkey
17. Hardpan lie
18. Ask Golf Guru (YT)
19. Australian Golf Union
20. Old driver heads vs today's
21. Myrtle Beach Golf Assoc.
22. Golf law
24. Ribbiting pond wildlife
25. Course owner change up for grab
26. Positive if winning. Also, golf balls bumpiness
27. Front nine on scorecard
28. Caddy advice not to go-for-it
29. Pro Robert Jones middle
31. Win vs rest of foursome
32. Pros love and ___ The Green Jacket
34. Ryder Cup PGA participant
35. EA Sports - maker of golf games stock ticker
39. Caddyshack Danny character
40. Georgia State Golf Foundation
41. "___ in the win", like fishing
42. Course hosting wedding, large car out front (short)
43. Bay Harbor Golf Club
44. PGA commish. considered ___ : Abbr
45. Player's health advisors: Abbr
46. Caddyshack's disorganized critique
47. No show golfer
50. Golfer who forgets clubs at home
52. Spit-shine your clubs
53. Fancy clubs and exquisite play
54. Event "extras" beyond core prize (slang)
55. Fans seen here
56. "Disc golfers do it in chains"

Down

1. Club part above the hosel
2. Watch golf in man-cave hideaway
3. Pro golfer Aoki
4. Heavy "beat-down" rain
5. Common activity after a round
6. Fee for tournament, and door purpose
7. 9 of the full 18 holes
8. Defined as "casual" water hazard, not perm.
9. Even pros are ___ of a bad day
10. Finger condition, hampers swing
11. PGA TOUR is, kinda, like other major sports
13. Temple Disc Golf Assoc.
14. Consume concession food quickly (slang)
15. Golfer unable to sum a scorecard
20. Your scorecard must be absolutely to count
21. Golf strategy requires gray ___
23. Pro Fay Crocker's NN
24. "Look out" in golf lingo
25. True Links courses, close to this
28. Didn't hear "FORE!"
30. Yardage, stat: Abbr
31. Brenden Stai Golf Classic
32. Nature's course dwellers
33. Has the NN - Crooner
34. United States Golf Teaching School
36. A cup does with the ball
37. Old driver head size vs today's biggies
38. Slow player (slang, animal)
40. Golf HDP Online Score Tracking System
42. Golf shoe tie
43. Masters Jacket, wool & poly ___
46. Course designer sketch
47. Arnold Palmer Golf Mng.
48. Slow golf, no interest
49. Win the four Majors is a grand ___
51. European Golf Assoc.

PUZZLE 39

Golf Fact: 67M to 1 - odds of making 2 hole-in-one / aces during the same round

Across

1. Long explosive drive (slang)

5. Legend of Bagger Vance movie, Damon

9. Gamblers must do with a scramble of stats

13. Akron District Golf Assoc.

14. Motorized course obstruction

15. Golf shirt & pant sets to other sports (short)

16. Grounds crew job

17. Golf course, an outdoor athletic ___

18. Mini golf wall is for this shot, also a money place

19. Blog post

21. Ignore that golf rule. Also, boot from event

23. Carbonated concession option

24. 18 holes = shot the ___ course

25. Total both shots ___ penalties in final score

28. Dangle sweet tourney invite

30. Course lounge drink, likely rum & water

32. Pro Thomas Dickson Armour, initially

33. High on your "self" when you win

37. Take in concession liquid

39. Course foliage, often a border

40. Popular pros have "charm" and "allure"

42. Lodewicus Theo "Louis" Oosthuizen initially

45. Diplomatic and International Golf Assoc.

46. Try to "solve" why you have ___ the yips (3wd)

48. Golf Channel show-er in Canada: Abbr

49. To sign your scorecard

51. 18 holes = 18 shots Scotch Whiskey???

54. Our green is ___ the group behind us. Also, those with eye troubles are ___ the obvious.

55. SA born pro Immelman's Masters Dinner menu

59. Story of Tiger's greatness

60. Power in power-cart

62. South Dakota Golf Assoc.

63. Aces

64. Course walkers are usually

65. Targets, stat: Abbr

66. SleepNumber, official ___ of golf tourneys

67. Directly in line to tee-off

68. Lay-up objective

Down

1. Alabama area (course), said by locals as (short)

2. Shoes give off, after a hot sweaty round

3. Mario Golf World Tour videogame

4. Uncomplicated swing

5. Golf became ___ more popular in 2000s

6. Fans are in, after seeing an amazing shot

7. Popular snack shack chicken food

8. Beginner-apprentice golfer

9. Equipment is, to USGA testing fac. for approval

10. Golf TV is seen where?

11. Ball washer finish

12. Calm fan disapproval

14. Larger putter head. Also a barrel-hammer

20. HOF pro Christy O'Connor

22. Golf bag hidden pockets purpose

25. Alberta Golf Superintendent Assoc.

26. Pro Nicholas Raymond Leige Price, initially

27. "Create" course plans, diagrams (slang)

29. Participants names placed in tourney structure

31. Golf legend descriptor

34. Sportswriter double-check

35. Clubhouse breakfast

36. "Cruel" swing feedback. Also, a medium range golfer

38. Staggered tee-times for course flow

41. Flags tourney AKA

43. Pro golfer NN - Terrible Tommy

44. Retired pros, player type

47. Complicit caddy for cheating golfer

49. Playing without friends

50. Beat after 18 holes

52. HOF Tommy Bolt

53. In broadcast booth

54. Chubby player (slang)

56. Toledo District Golf Assoc.

57. Irish Golf Teachers Federation

58. Drive hard, putt w ___

61. Access to see tourney (short)

PUZZLE 40

1	2	3	4			5	6	7	8		9	10	11	12
13					14						15			
16					17						18			
19				20			21		22					
		23					24							
25	26	27			28		29							
30			31		32				33			34	35	36
37				38						39				
40					41		42	43	44		45			
		46			47							48		
	49	50					51		52	53				
54						55				56	57	58
59				60		61				62			
63				64						65			
66				67						68			

Golf Fact: The sand wedge was invented by pro golfer Gene Sarazen

Across

1. TOUR's Stuff-We-All-Get
5. American Singles Golf Assoc.
9. Modern Woods material carbon ___
14. Golden Tee arcade
15. Indoor putting machine rug
16. Sunrise game
17. Houses tourney registry
19. PGA TOUR, most titles
20. The Whites, tees
21. "Golf" retailer, goes on and on
23. After round chowed down
24. Part of OOB fencing
25. Clean-up the rules
27. Stiffen grip
30. Putt longer than flag stick, bet, game
31. Golf lessons
32. Knuth NN - ___ of the Slope
33. Ladies tee box marker
37. Good Government Golf Tourney
38. Balls innards
39. PGA Vice President (slang)
40. Balls package
41. Course wildlife. Add an "S"
42. Luck of the Draw game insp.
43. Golf magazine gets around
45. Flakey golfer
46. Sam Snead NN
49. Concession food toppings
50. S. Califonia course locale (part of)
51. Course customer protector: Abbr
52. Speed golf essential
56. Play ___ the sun goes down
58. Birth of a tourney
60. 2 HOF w Pinehurst HOF
61. Player bodies do it poorly
62. Sawbill Frisbee Golf Assoc.
63. Charity golf tourney, often
64. Low-brow golf joke
65. Unwashed golf attire

Down

1. Scottish Golf Environment Group
2. "OK" to hit signal
3. Pre round prayer, ending
4. "Links" for non-links course
5. Find a ball
6. Turtleneck green AKA
7. And juice, clubhouse drink
8. NW USA course wildlife
9. Suitable for north courses
10. Golfer Poulter
11. Awarded to winner (slang)
12. Pros "lift" fan spirits
13. PGA cup, Europe vs USA
18. Follow the leader
22. ESPN documentary telling
26. Hitting ball over water feeling
27. Savannah Disc Golf Club
28. Three Rivers Golf Assoc.
29. Carts (slang)
30. Ed Oliver NN
32. N. Canada course resident
34. ___ out the win
35. Tourney detail (slang)
36. Seniors/Legends TOUR players
38. Half of pro-am part. (short)
42. Divot tool
44. Power cart man. ID
45. Collection of golf holes
46. Prolonged bad play
47. Golfing single
48. Turf type for hitting balls
49. Course fee increase, no benefit
53. Tourney details
54. Northern Counties Golf Union
55. Golf equipment
57. Idaho Golf Assoc.
59. Mpumalanga Golf Union

PUZZLE 41

1	2	3	4		5	6	7	8		9	10	11	12	13
14					15					16				
17			18							19				
20							21	22				23		
			24				25			26				
27	28	29				30								
31					32					33	34	35	36	
37				38						39				
40				41					42					
			43	44				45						
46	47	48					49							
50				51			52				53	54	55	
56			57		58	59								
60					61					62				
63					64					65				

Golf Fact: PGA TOUR first started in 1929

Across

1. Crowd action
5. Of ground, flies after contact
9. Ohio Public Golf Assoc.
13. Achievement
14. Tourney's fiery starter, may be from gun
15. Club to ball, like a hammer
16. Carolina Senior Golf Assoc.
17. Tiger's had a ___ with the law
18. Golf course obstacle
19. He will golf if John does not
21. Summer activity, not golfing
23. Grounds crew top-dressing
24. Yardage from reds
25. Golf Fights Cancer
28. Municipal course open to the ___ public
30. High ball flights
32. PGA post-Tiger, a whole new (time)
33. Informs all about your cheating
37. Caddyshack's hit music single release v film
39. PGA TOUR, has most titles
40. Power cart manufacturer ID
42. Tiger's sixth sense (short)
45. Boston area courses, US locale
46. Tee off honors go ___
48. Happy Gilmore awarder
49. Accidental ball tap = this stroke penalty
51. Disc golf "putt"
54. A golf cart's purpose
55. PGA TOUR changed name to, briefly
59. Tin Cup, female lead Russo
60. ___ ist brand balls and equipment
62. Swing with it = success. Not hard
63. Tour player accommodations
64. Each hole tee-off has it
65. Elderly Gentlemens' Golf Society
66. Vegas on golf gambling win
67. Study green
68. Front 9 to overall round

Down

1. Certified Golf Course Superintendent
2. Ball unfound in 3-minutes, ruling
3. Asian American Golf Association
4. Course designer sketches
5. Missed Tee-time
6. Pro golfer Poulter
7. Interest in golf without Tiger
8. 50yr+ PGA event
9. Golf bet usually has money ___ (3wd)
10. Golf's 1st Olympics, 1900
11. Driver head-size as of late
12. AUS women's tour: Abbr
14. Edge of green
20. Driving Accuracy, stat
22. Majestic course flyers, found in pond
25. Wide opening
26. Links course ground plays very ___
27. Pro golfer home (slang)
29. Some golfer's 'person'alized drivers
31. Hardness of golf ball
34. Ryder Cup grouping
35. Caddyshack's Knight, Chase, Murray etc
36. Golf Channel's feed to newer TV's
38. Course redos
41. Power-cart's GPS screen
43. Paid course fees
44. Course dress policy
47. ___ from work to play more golf
49. Golf course, an open-air athletic ___
50. Caddyshack's star caddy name
52. Scoring Average. stat
53. Fees at well known course go up high
54. Out of cart fumble
56. Omaha Amputee Golf Assoc.
57. United States Golf Register
58. Between holes relax
61. Thomas Dickson Armour, initially

PUZZLE 42

Golf Fact: PGA TOUR consists of 245 players

Across

1. Bungle the ball
5. Less athletic golf bod
9. Green w center as high point
14. The Justin of the PGA
15. Pro with NN - The Tower
16. Avoid work, play golf
17. Asian Golf Industry Federation
18. Raveneaux Ladies Golf Assoc.
19. Golfer about to crack top 10
20. No hazard & no trees course design
22. Course outhouse
24. To put names on trophy
25. PGA post-Tiger, a new (time)
26. Pro-Am participant
27. 18 holes is enough to ___ a golfer's craving
32. Old moth ___ golf clothes
34. Caddies are paid
35. Lone loss on scorecard
36. Maker / supplier of golf equipment. Also time zone - Greenwich Mean Time
37. PGA's new Texas HQ, in 2022
41. Gang of golfers
44. Golfing vet (slang)
46. Power-cart rester
47. Tennessee Golf Assoc.
48. Tourney watchers and supporters
52. French golf hat
56. Slick grips for gameplay
57. European Innovative golf rake, brand
58. Golf Greens Fore U
60. Pro Julius Boros NN
61. Express problem w the rule
62. Bag carry
63. Crowd does w noise
64. A 4th to our 4-some
65. 1980's Mattel - Golf maker for kids
66. Mini golf, young persons together time

Down

1. Best scorecard, put in display on wall
2. Golf app access point
3. Club from bag, purpose
4. Tee-off honors means to
5. Power cart AKA
6. Crowd will hoot & ___
7. Ultra Korte Golf
8. Privileges or members vs non members
9. Play different today
10. Nike renowned R&D facility in TX, name
11. ID on a ball
12. Extreme Disc Golf Experience
13. Course buck
21. Player on the team
23. Early course these were sheep wallow
28. Iron Club (short)
29. Scottish Blind Golf Society
30. Hall place, for pros
31. Your Golf Travel
32. William Mehlhorn middle
33. Barren course
35. Mark Francis O'Meara, initially
38. Sunrise, Sunset times check (short)
39. Clubhouse rented room chow
40. Old Ladies Golf Assoc.
41. Nutty snack when watching game
42. Tee time reservation, a form of
43. Range ball decoration
45. Natural talent can't be
46. "Smartly dressed" for the round
49. Presidential golf, no-show
50. Clean hit w less backspin (slang)
51. Florida, most courses per
52. Connecticut State Golf Assoc.
53. Original balls, ___ wooden object
54. Caddyshack Chase's character's golf status
55. Pro Knuth NN - ___ of the Slope
59. Golf Environment Org.

PUZZLE 43

Golf Fact: Charles Kocsis, in 1931 was the youngest ever winner on the PGA TOUR at 18 years, 6 months and 9 days

Across

1. Long Drivers of America
4. Golf games are streamed from it
7. 2 events, same wkd. gives a watcher what?
9. Needed for "FORE's"
10. Buick Open golf tourney
12. Must be to shoot smartly
13. Improves anyone's score
15. Course maintenance
17. US Open fairway descriptor
18. Wire around a closed course area
19. PGA Championship
21. LPGA golfer Lorie K.
22. Hot-wired a cart, drove away
24. Player's practice and improve their skill
25. Worst.....round..... ___
26. Drops a "found it" ball
28. A cart's speed governor function
30. Tops your outfit
32. Sand hazard (slang)
35. Pro card must contain, or penalties abound
39. Carts quiet cat-like engines
40. Collegiate golf body
42. 1936 PGA Championship win, Shute
44. CLE course water neighbor
45. Fans, off the bandwagon
46. Almost Professional Golf Assoc.
47. Happy about golf
49. Course playing field, AKA
52. Mock, annoy your buddies swing
53. Common thing to do after a round
54. Yard, stat: Abbr
55. Pro William Casper's middle
56. Pro Lloyd Mangrum's middle
57. Fast green condition
58. Offensive golfer

Down

1. Pros play attracts "adorable" affection from fans
2. It's keeping you away from snack shack
3. 140-180 ___ s make up a typical 18-hole course
4. Ben Hogan NN (3wd)
5. Pros on tour ___ their spot, it is not given
6. Tourney structure
7. Foot uniform for golf
8. Pro's NN - Lumpy
10. Carabiner (short)
11. Tee off hierarchy
12. Hotel to course movers
14. Dull golf pencil needs it
16. Sub Par Holes
17. Late for tee-time feeling
20. Friend for a round
23. European Amateur Golf Tour
27. Q-school grad, result
29. Apple device can play golf recording
31. Tied golf shoes
32. Put English on that drive
33. Masters date, Astrology sign
34. Water proofed golf shoe
36. Well studied golfer
37. Hit by golf ball, result
38. A cart go'er
39. Feel in your step when shooting well
41. 4-some back-up golfer (short)
43. 2009 PGA Championship win, Yong Eun
48. Course BBQ cooking, just the outside
50. Lessons purpose (short)
51. Rhode Island Golf Assoc.

PUZZLE 44

Golf Fact: The first Ryder Cup was held in 1927

Across

1. Short game shot
5. Disc Golf Course Review
9. Head cover material supplier
12. Pros shine, past tense
13. Northern Ohio course water neighbor
14. Dubai based golf tour
16. ___ ist brand
17. Tournament place
18. Scottish Blind Golf Society
19. Carry, time ___
20. Range basket accident
22. Power-cart driving on green
23. Fan reaction to bad call
24. Course walkers are usually
27. WMF use of "minigolf", not miniature
29. All over the place golfer
31. Golf course event room rental, UK
32. Never use club may feel
33. Bushes w balls (slang)
36. Pond wildlife
37. Course maintenance
39. Craig Robert Stadler, initially
40. Katharine Hepburn in golf film "Pat & Mike"
41. Tires on a golf power-cart
45. Short shot - ___ dip (slang)
46. Golf hat, head locale
48. Sweaty golf clothes rub result
50. Pro's NN - Robopro
52. Pro Liselotte Neumann's NN
53. Hammer towel to bag
56. Mini golf's untainted fun
57. Disc golf disc's beveled ___ rim
58. Old gas power cart (short) (slang)
59. These "pipes" help power shots
60. Running golf game essential
61. Dansk Golf Union
62. Practice swing
63. Presidents golf a lot during theirs

Down

1. Confident golfer
2. Sketchy hole-in-one claim. Also a balloon
3. Place ball, with target
4. Teammate AKA
5. Sweet meal at snack shack
6. Problem with a rule
7. Municipal course patron
8. " ___ in the win", like fishing
9. Meds on sidelines: Abbr
10. All the pro e-stats are here
11. PGA broadcast language (short)
12. A "mix" of reactions from Tiger gossip
15. Putting is main ___ of mini golf
21. 4 in a group
23. Pro's NN - Jelly
25. Wind weather, not for golfing
26. Hat sharing risk
28. Angle between shaft and bottom
30. Club handle refurbish
33. PGA CEO Waugh
34. Player who invokes bet "press"
35. Pro William Mehlhorn's middle
37. Moving upward on leaderboard
38. Physical presence
39. Bingo Bango Bongo reward, on green, to cup. Like KP
42. Army golf group
43. Bob hits, then Carl. "Carl"
44. Notoriety of golf fame
47. Golf words
49. Playing from the Blues, for avg golfer
51. Garcia, 2007 CA Championship, into cup controversy
52. Ball unfound in 3-minutes, ruling
54. Contract benefit
55. Caddyshack movie, caddy manager

PUZZLE 45

Golf Fact: Nick Faldo's 58 in 2016 was the lowest ever PGA TOUR round - Travelers Championship

Across

1. Atmospheric condition

5. A cheater is ___ player, usually

9. Done at a driving range, for a stall

10. Cheap course grub

13. Stories of Tiger's greatness

14. Kick wedge contacts

15. Cola offering

16. Quantity of beers drank during round

17. Golf bag pockets purpose. Think war

19. Furthest tee-off area (slang)

22. Golf Channel's box display, old TVs

23. Facial reaction after long putt

24. Citation on a contract (short)

25. Wrong club used: Abbr

26. Golf hat to head

27. Maraging in clubs, ___ in bike frames

28. Golfer reaction after big loss

30. "Setup" to win

33. USA in Ryder Cup

36. Drinking hole

39. Elm's resist it with ease

42. Course's black bird, AKA

43. "Looping" mini golf hole

45. Craig Robert Stadler, initially

47. S. Califonia course locale (part of)

48. Course prices show an "increase"

49. Tourney's novelty check - cannot what?

51. Wrap hands on grip

53. 2v2 paired scoring

54. Mini golf water hazard

55. Scottish Blind Golf Society

57. Unwashed golf socks

58. Toronto footballer in Pro-Am (short)

59. Augusta is former fruitland ___

60. Old clubhouse rodents

61. HOF to St. Augustine

62. Pros take a game ___ serious

Down

1. Course card documenters

2. Henry Cotton NN

3. Caddyshack crew at work

4. #1 pro mid-range golf disc

5. Corey Pavin's middle

6. Gets ball out of rough, no stroke

7. Golf blog post, AKA

8. Caddyshack II reception

9. Old golf shoes condition

10. Water surrounding green does this

11. Golf joke reaction: Abbr

12. Tourney watchers, live

18. New year, ___ of clubs

20. Adjustable equip will have

21. Weather, not for golfing

23. On w 2 shots to par (slang)

27. Contract upping

29. Fan drink

31. Ball on cart path, ruled

32. PGA's Dana Quigley to Brett

34. Spanish tourney prize

35. Hold in after bad shot

37. Dana Quigley NN

38. Friendly game

40. Q School, qualifier

41. 3 top golfers

44. Having ___ of the yips

46. Craig Stadler NN

48. Modern push cart's may have

50. Pro shop is one

52. Ladies Amateur Golf Assoc.

53. Southern Golf Tours, LLC

56. Course buffet garb

PUZZLE 46

Golf Fact: Tiger has spent the most weeks as golf's world's number #1 at 281

Across

1. Dutch Golf Perf. Institute
5. A cheater is ___ player, usually
9. Ball into sand or water, comical description
14. Range btw 16° and 65°
15. Periodic power-cart "up" needed
16. Native golfers
17. Player wives
18. Caddyshack movie's dialogue piece
19. Tiger's had a ___ with the law
20. Caddyshack's Murray's no-prep character
22. High and low green
24. Big ___ Disc Golf (BDDG)
26. Beers after round & course after completion
27. Ball on hard ground
30. Pre round prayer, ending
31. Tee off honors go ___
32. Say your score again
36. Golf joke reaction: Abbr
37. Course field greenery
38. "Expand" hole yardage
43. Tourney medical is under
47. "50 ft putt" is a tall one
48. Carts are easy enough for a child to ___
49. House and grounds of a course, description
52. 2nd set of clubs
53. Rumors about Tiger cause "shame" and ___
55. Sharp game in course lounge
59. Hips & shoulders generate
60. Barren course
62. Changes in game's "flow"
63. Golf course, an outdoor athletic ___
64. Golf Ball on opening shot is "set"
65. Erie District Golf Assoc.
66. Caddyshack's Danny character descriptor
67. PGA, no ___
68. Golf TV signed one w Tiger

Down

1. Diplomatic and International Golf Assoc.
2. Q-School finisher (short)
3. Golf Ch. often conducts a "viability question"
4. Has first-hand knowledge of pro golfer news
5. Georgia municipal course place: Abbr
6. Course actionist
7. Poke fun at a friend's shot, may ___ friend
8. Hit it long AKA
9. Range ball design marks
10. Decent golfer
11. Early golf clubs shaft-head joiner thread
12. Accept course rules
13. Where the front-9 is but a memory
21. Golf ball descriptor, and a smooth head
23. Losing "a few" balls
25. Stiff wind may cause ball's flight to ___
27. Comes up from course buffet's spicy food
28. Tiger rumors, often ___ ymous
29. Golden Tee game controller, a ___ ball
30. HOF pro Allan Robertson
33. Hot golf market, continent
34. Eldrick "Tiger" Woods middle
35. Tee box boundary
39. Tiger's dominance in 2021, likely (3wd)
40. 1774's first golf champion
41. "Elation" from round win, & dancing TV show
42. HOF pro Ernie Els
43. PGA TOUR in USA vs other tours
44. PGA a-ok w this gov't body: Abbr
45. Caddyshack's Danny character descriptor
46. Golf shoe, water "proofed"
50. Result
51. Pro Isao Aoki NN
52. Pro shop buy-all
54. Skill needed to total score
56. Passenger gets to in a power-cart
57. Temple Disc Golf Assoc.
58. "Lock" bag in locker
59. Taiwanese born PGA pro C.T.
61. Vegas gambling O ___

PUZZLE 47

Golf Fact: FedEx Cup winner takes home
$10 Million in prize money

Across

1. Golf trivia fail
6. Good Government Golf Tourney
10. Eases sun burn
14. Originally a course clubhouse was a "big home"
15. Hogan's surrounding intimidation feel
16. Pro Jan Stephenson's NN
17. Course map AKA
18. Golfers do it over small hazards
19. Certified Golf Course Superintendent
20. To "sign" your scorecard
22. Happy Gilmore's indoor scenes filmed here
24. Playing from reds, distance
26. Pulled on naive golfer
29. Sum of score
34. English Golf Unions
35. Players visor design
38. Heated golf discussion over ruling
39. Barren course
41. Lay-up = short of what full shot ___ reach
43. Southern Illinois Golf Assoc.
44. Par is ___ 70 for US Open, usually
46. Press "mixes" up Tiger facts to create controversies
48. Pro Larry Gene Nelson, initially
49. Old pro earnings vs today's are ___ -tiny
50. Inheriting golf partner
52. Golf time-share pitch purpose
56. Alluring & beautiful golfer
60. Leave tourney
64. "Spot" on hole
65. Pro Gene Littler's middle
67. Pro Helen Alfredsson's NN
68. Power-cart without charge
69. Compose then "email" a fan letter to pro
70. Tease & ___ friend about their tattered-like swing
71. Barely ___ out the win
72. Visor hider
73. Pro Hubert Green's middle

Down

1. Salute Military Golf Assoc.
2. Too-tight golf shirt
3. Stroke, each is a scoring ___
4. Most pro golfers victory demeanor
5. Steps prepping for a stroke
6. Female golfer
7. A member pays a lower green fee than "non-member"
8. Part of course drainage filter
9. A tourney's luxury box food offering
10. PGA hedging, insur ___
11. Game streaming troubles, sometimes
12. Tee box hit-per-hole
13. Boston course are in this area of U.S.A.
21. Liquid from concession, goes well with gin
23. Golf Tourney Assoc. of America
25. Course redos (short)
26. Post round event
27. Gamblers OK the terms
28. Where rich watch live golf
30. PGA pros have fine ones
31. Course walkers are usually
32. Pro golfer NN - Miss Sluggs
33. Pros Crocker & O'Hair
36. Club selection influenced by it
37. Caddyshack's Judge Smail's first name
40. 10,000 golf hours, McLaughlin
42. Feeling when shooting near water & then losing sight of ball
45. E-scorecard input
47. Disc golf flick shot
51. Golf TV shows tourney again
53. Delete score
54. Pro NN - Radar
55. Caddyshack movie, each film segment
56. Club is "constructed"
57. Cleveland course water neighbor
58. Lost ball exploration action
59. Beginners clubs are made with extra "size"
61. Alumni and Fan Golf Assoc.
62. Golf joke was a laugh ___ (lawless)
63. Golf tourney temporary structure
66. Stores golf media: Abbr

PUZZLE 48

1	2	3	4	5		6	7	8	9		10	11	12	13
14						15					16			
17						18					19			
20				21		22			23				
		24			25							
26	27	28							29	30	31	32	33
34				35			36	37		38		
39			40		41				42		43	
44				45		46				47		48	
49							50			51		
			52	53	54	55					
56	57	58	59					60			61	62	63
64					65		66		67			
68					69				70			
71					72				73			

Golf Fact: Nick Faldo and Danny Willed are the only 2 Englishmen to win the Masters

Across

1. Course top mng (short)
5. To sign your scorecard
11. Starters horn
12. Below average course rating
14. Funky golf hat
15. Rocky mountain course
16. Pull cart storage
17. Wooden pegs
18. Richmond Golf Assoc.
19. Master's winner " ___ dreaming?"
20. "Emailed" the membership
21. Golf bag appearance structure. Also basketball players defining feature
22. Pro's madness, shouting at Caddy
24. ___ clubs, balls and beers....for a fun round
25. Store bag in "mesh locker"
26. European Disabled Golf Assoc.
27. 1969 PGA Championship course: Abbr
28. Mud all over club head. Also, baked
29. Lawrence Park Golf Services
31. Play-through request answer
32. Distort ball
34. Event audio equipment, hi- ___
35. Ottawa Disc Golf Club
39. Player wives, derogatory
40. Shots AKA
41. Sinkable putt vicinity
42. Really "punch" the ball
43. Early season skin tone
44. Golfers, for the lead
45. Worn around neck on Maui course
46. Links green undulation
47. Golf glove permanence, dirt or rubber
50. Weather on course conditions
52. Electronic scoring method
53. Play different today
54. Mini Golf narrow path, obstacle
55. Hit the target "straight on"
56. Water hazard plant life

Down

1. Club behind ball on ground at address
2. John Daly, 23 - highest ever
3. Cleveland course water neighbor
4. Grass crew main. supply
5. Lift flagstick while player putts
6. How pro's stay in contact w fans
7. Kick wedge contactors
8. Tiger's sixth sense (short)
9. Pack away your clubs
10. Disorganized golf net
11. Broadcasted golf, by e.g. satellite
13. Grass is turf is not
14. Unscared golfers tough-out any weather
15. Swingers try to alter ball with arm movements
20. Bleacher divisions (short)
21. Contend, compete with.... at the tourney
23. Tiger has natural "ability"
24. Nederlands Neurologen Golf Kamp.
25. Power-cart is a mini one of these
28. Potty-mouth golfer verbiage
30. Streaming golf match devices: Abbr
31. Tournament "place". Also, golf.com, web ___
32. Golf Cart vehicle type
33. Pull cart does for weight on shoulder
34. Failing golf course ___ chapter eleven
36. Evil golfer
37. Pros NN - Two Gloves
38. Fairway high point
40. Ready golf objective
42. It is said that legend Ben Hogan ___ green
43. Towel, ___ bag like a tail and a donkey
46. Done with Golf Digest
47. Top golfer of the PGA, like top actor in film
48. "50 ft putt", always a tall one
49. Skill to compete, competent
51. S. Florida municipal course locale (short)

PUZZLE 49

Golf Fact: An average of 3.6 million people tune into the PGA TOUR coverage of a tourney

Across

1. Do to manicure greens grass
5. Makes 1 beer last the entire round
9. Scott Macpherson Golf Design
13. Junior golfer problem
14. Pro Shop
15. Your score, after lessons
16. Mario Golf Toadstool Tour, videogame
17. Pro shop merch, still has the ___
18. Holds a golf course's loan - a mortg___
19. Narrowly avoid a bogey
21. Study putt-line error
23. Golfer oration about lousy performance
24. Extra ball holder
25. Golf Fights Cancer, charity
28. "Golf" news show on the Golf Channel
30. High ball flights
32. Legend Ben Hogan, best in his
33. Black vs gold tee yardage difference
37. PGA Championship wkd is ___ to Memorial Day
39. Sign - "No spikes upon ___ " & door function
40. Power-cart manufacturers ID
42. Tiger's sixth sense: Abbr
45. Wind weather force, affects golfing
46. Tee off honors is your group's drives ___
48. Alternative to sports drink (alcoholic)
49. Accidental ball tap, stroke penalty
51. Wind test grass action
54. A golf cart's purpose
55. PGA TOUR changed name, briefly, to what?
59. Golf movie, Tin Cup female lead, Russo
60. Titleist, from " ___ holder"
62. International Golf Psychology Assoc.
63. Tour player accommodations
64. Ready golf or honors, tee-off ___
65. Bruising injury, major side effect
66. Vegas does on gambling win
67. Golf term for "learn" and "study" the green
68. Pros Green & Venturi

Down

1. Records the tour action (short)
2. Royal Canadian Golf Assoc.
3. Golf tourney airing
4. Pro Padraig Harrington's middle
5. Driving range helps this level of golfer
6. Institute Of Golf
7. "Persuade" him into taking lessons. Also, a golfing app directions pop-up
8. The "old" American ___ Golf Assoc.
9. Scoring well, star-like feeling. Also, carbonated water
10. PGA TOUR Par 4 ace in 2001
11. A tee-to-hole distance on a Par 5
12. Course owner possesses this legal document
14. Golfers have a wide or narrow one
20. HOF pro Peter Alliss
22. Golf tourney pro pay ___ . Also a weigh device
25. Wide opening
26. Ground pack under the green
27. Pro golfer home (slang)
29. Some golfer's 'person'alized drivers
31. "Hardness" of golf ball AKA
34. Golf Tourney Assoc. of America
35. Life would be a living one, without golf
36. Golf course obstacle
38. Course redos (short)
41. Cart's GPS screen
43. Paid course fees
44. Golfer of intermediate skill
47. ___ to play golf (time of life)
49. Golf course, an athletic ___
50. Caddyshack star caddy
52. Scoring Average
53. Ask ball to drop and stay (slang)
54. Triple Bogey (slang)
56. Fans at pros
57. Ball lands here, on green
58. Old clubhouse rodents
61. Thomas Dickson Armour initials

PUZZLE 50

1	2	3	4			5	6	7	8		9	10	11	12
13					14						15			
16					17						18			
19				20				21		22				
			23					24						
25	26	27			28		29							
30			31		32				33			34	35	36
37				38						39				
40					41		42	43	44		45			
			46			47						48		
	49	50						51		52	53			
54						55					56	57	58	
59				60		61				62				
63				64						65				
66				67						68				

Golf Fact: Steve Stricker's -33 at the 2009 Bob Hope Classic was the lowest ever tourney score in relation to par

PUZZLE 1

```
G R A D   A B E D     B E S A D
R U S E   R A K E     E X T R A
O B S T A C L E S     H E A R T
G E N E R A L   C P A   T O E
      R E D S   R E V I E W S
S A T I N Y   B I D E N
O C H O A   A L B A   C C D G
F E A R   S T E E L   O H I O
A S I A   C O N S   P R O V E
    T R E N D   D A P P E R
S A M E O N E   R E P O
A G E   L E T   A M E R I C A
V I R A L   I G N O R A M U S
E L I T E   M A G E   T G T S
D E T E R   E Y E D   E A S T
```

PUZZLE 2

```
O N E S     F G L F   D S G A
M O S T   F L A I L   E T A S
I P P A   I A G T O   L O T S
T E N D I N G   T W O I R O N
    S G E G   L I N G E R
E T H   S E V E N T H
G R I P   T D A   G A T H E R
G E N E S   G   P E A C E
S E T T L E   U P S   D R O P
    T E N S E U P   D N S
  S P E E C H   T R G A
S T A R T L E   T I T L I S T
E A T S   O R I O N   A N T I
E R I E   S P O U T   R F I D
N E O N   E A G T   M O R E
```

PUZZLE 3

```
H I T S   I G A F   T G C S A
A G E E   N O N O   R O L E X
R O A M   T O D O   A B O V E
S T R I P E S   T W I S T E D
H A S N O N E   I G N
    A S S N   T H E J O H N
  A G R E E   F E R V I D
A M A         A D S
I M P A C T   S C A L E
R O S A L E S   C H A T
    I N N   L I K A B L E
A T L A N T A   O N E I R O N
P R I N T   C G S I   L A S T
P I N T O   K E E N   O V E R
T O K E N   S N D G   R O R Y
```

PUZZLE 4

```
    T A B       L O P
  T H E R U N   G A L A   R G
R O A R E D     D I N N E R
U P G R A D E   M I N T A G E
T D G A   G A O E   H I R E
S O L I D   D U D S   E V E N
  G E N U S   D E M A R E T
      S I M I L A R
M U S T N O T   N I G H T
C A N T   G R O G   D R O O P
A S I A   L O R E   A L B A
S H O R T E N   E D I B L E S
T I N L I D   U P B E A T
E E   E V A N   D E P A R T
    T O Y     T A R
```

PUZZLE 5

```
H A L E . F A C T . A G C .
R E L A Y . A L O E . B R R R
I R A T E . S T U N . E A S E
C O S T S . T E N T H . V . J
H I K E . P O R T . A G I L E
. C A R B O N . E R R A T I C
. . E W E . R A D I A N T . .
. P R O V E . T E N S E . . .
L I E W E L L . F I S . . . .
I N T E L L I . R O T A T E .
T E A S E . T H I N . D A R T
T . I . D A T E S . S H I N Y
L E N D . S L A B . N E W E R
E V E N . S E V E . E R A S E
. E R A . T R E E . S E N T .
```

PUZZLE 6

```
D I R T . . W . . S P A T .
L E M A . G M A C . P U R E
E V A N . F A G A . A N T E
D I G I T U P . B A C K I N G
B L I T H E . L I T E . C A L
Y E N . E L N I N O . O L G A
. D E M O . M E N S T E E S .
B . A R C H I T E C T . . S .
E M P T Y O U T . O O P S . .
S E A T . B R E W E R . R T G
A D S . B R R R . R E T I R E
D I S P L A Y . C A R A V A N
C A R E . U N I S . L A N E .
A G E S . P I N E . L T D S .
L E S S . . N . . E Y E S .
```

PUZZLE 7

```
S C A N . C H U B . B E N C H
P A P A . H E R O . E L I H U
U S G T . A L B A . V E N U E
R E C U R . P A R S E V E N .
. . R E S I N . A L A S K A .
S T R A P I N . D I E T . . .
P R O L O N G . A D D E D U P
E G O . . . . . . . A S I . .
C A T T R A P . S P L U R G E
. R A G S . H O O T E R S . .
S T R I P E . P I V O T . . .
. R E V I S I O N . T E R M S
R A P I D . S L I T . R U B E
I D E A L . B O N D . L S G A
B E L L Y . N S G A . Y E A R
```

PUZZLE 8

```
R E C U R . A L C C . A S G A
A D O R E . H I G H . P G A C
G U I L D . A N C E . P A W N
S C L A F F . E S A S T A K E
. . . T O L E R A T E . . . .
E M P E R O R . . . G R A S S
S E O . D O R A L . A L L A N
T D R P . D O M E D . F O R E
E A T E N . R I V E R . N G A
S L A T E . . E M E R G E D .
. . . S T A L L O N E . . . .
W E L L T O D O . S T A T E S
A R E A . R I G A . A S I D E
R I M S . Z O O M . L O D G E
N E A T . A S S T . S N A C K
```

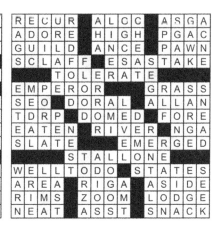

PUZZLE 9

```
SWAT    SHREWD
 STARE   TOUGHEN
ELEVEN WILLGIVE
REPEAT AGEE  NIX
RED   BUMS  FEAT
OVAL  LAGA  SORT
REDO  ASH  CURSE
   ONCE  BONE
 HAPPY MEN  SCRG
 OVER  DOTE TOOL
SLED  GOVS   ABA
EER  GONE SISTER
GOAROUND  ASPIRE
LUGGAGE   PAINT
 TEASED   SONG
```

PUZZLE 10

```
BARS   GEMS  NANA
ABET  DONOT  IDOL
GALA  EAGLE  GOTO
STYLISH  DL THREE
   ERIE  ELATED
CGF   SANDALS
ARID  TDA  REPEAT
RANIT   M   SOLVE
TAKEIN EDO  TGIC
  INORDER   ASH
 MANGLE   SNES
SOLHEIM SECTION
ONTO  MOWER  ROLE
REEL  IVORY  UNIT
TYRE  TENT   TENS
```

PUZZLE 11

```
CLAN  ISAO  SIGHT
HOME  SCAN  ERROR
ERICCLOSE  CEASE
FEDERAL  CRU  TEA
  SEND  HARDEST
CLASSD  POLEE
MERIT  TRIP  SFGA
OMIT  TEACH  COAX
NADA  RENE  FRAME
  TRACK  PRIMED
SCREECH  PLOP
CHA  CEO RENTALS
RINSE  IDENTICAL
ALGID  COST  ONCE
PIECE  EASY  NEED
```

PUZZLE 12

```
HUFF   PICS  BOBS
ANAL  BASIC  ERIE
TIDA  ASTRO  NAGA
STEWART  CRITTER
  SAKI  LEGGED
AMP   EMPEROR
LOAD  REP  STATES
ALTER   G   ASIDE
SEESAW IFS  SEGA
  INAPRIL   SAM
 MAGGIE  RICH
BENNETT MCGAVIN
IDGA  IRATE  NAME
DIET  NOTED  DSGA
SALE  GLEE   SEAT
```

PUZZLE 13

```
DEED   SHIP   SCALE
EASE   LAGA   POLEY
TGTS   ENCY   INONE
ELECTED   FITNESS
RESERVE   ENT
   NEED   ENLARGE
 DATES   SERIAL
LAB        BLK
DRAWAL   BRASS
RETREAT   SLOT
   RIO   CAPABLE
ANDMORE   ONEIRON
LOADS   CORK   LAST
BONGO   AGEE   OVER
ANGEL   PART   RORY
```

PUZZLE 14

```
    CRO     MAC
  SCRAPE  FARR  NE
BERATE     KEISER
ELEMENT   LEATHER
ADAM   UNIS   TODO
NOTES   BONA   EVER
  MEDIA   DESIRED
     DRAINED
  DIRECTV   TOPIT
BIKE   HOOT   LEGAL
EEKS   INTO   CURE
AGITATE   PACKAGE
REMOVE    JOINER
DL   RICH   NATNAT
   EST     RSG
```

PUZZLE 15

```
MEAL   GLOB   AWT
DANCE   IONE   META
ASGCA   LUGE   SBGS
SHAUN   FIRST  S   P
HUGS   ROSE   AGILE
 PEEPER   ERRATIC
  ADD   NEGLECT
 SCORE    TEASE
BLANKET   CAT
AIRTIME   LISTEN
SPOON   ECON   ONES
K  L  GENES   HOGAN
EDIT   GALE   UNITE
TENN   AGES   LINES
 FAT   DEBT   KEEN
```

PUZZLE 16

```
COGS    K     AREA
GONE   ASIA   WAGL
GLEE   MITT   ASGM
CLOSEUP   AIRHEAD
SEVENS   LITE   DNA
ACE   DEFILE   GOAT
 TREE   COMMENCE
R   GAGPERSON    S
OFFGREEN   DECI
BIAS   NASSAU   END
OGR   RUSE   GLANCE
TURNESA   WRESTLE
REAL   NIKE   GRIT
ELGA   TIDE   CANS
SLAY    I     GALE
```

PUZZLE 17

T	O	F	U		D	R	E	D		A	S	G	C	A
E	L	I	N		M	A	G	E		S	T	O	O	L
N	I	N	E		L	W	G	A		P	R	I	N	T
S	N	E	A	D		L	E	F	T	H	A	N	D	
		R	A	P	I	D		H	A	N	G	O	N	
F	L	A	T	T	E	N		B	A	L	D			
P	E	R	H	A	P	S		H	I	T	S	O	N	G
G	A	M								T	E	A		
A	N	Y	C	L	U	B		O	N	E	S	T	A	R
		H	O	S	S		V	I	C	T	O	R	Y	
V	A	C	A	T	E		M	A	N	O	R			
	P	O	R	T	R	A	I	T		N	E	V	E	R
I	R	A	T	E		S	A	I	D		T	I	D	E
L	O	S	E	R		S	M	O	G		C	L	U	E
E	N	T	R	Y		T	I	N	T		H	E	C	K

PUZZLE 18

S	T	U	M	P		G	G	G	T		S	A	N	G
M	A	N	O	R		A	U	R	A		O	B	E	Y
G	U	I	D	E		L	E	A	P		R	E	A	R
A	T	T	E	S	T		S	T	A	G	E	T	T	E
			S	H	O	R	T	E	S	T				
F	A	S	T	O	N	E				A	D	U	L	T
R	G	A		T	I	N	G	E		A	R	N	I	E
O	I	L	S		C	O	U	L	D		V	I	S	A
S	L	E	E	T		S	T	I	R	S		T	A	R
T	E	S	T	Y			H	E	I	R	E	S	S	
			P	E	R	S	U	A	D	E				
M	E	S	M	E	R	I	C		D	E	P	A	R	T
A	R	E	A		A	L	E	C		A	L	F	I	E
D	I	E	S		S	E	N	T		R	A	G	O	N
E	E	K	S		E	Y	E	S		M	Y	A	T	T

PUZZLE 19

	W	H	A	P		A	F	R	I	C	A	
	M	O	O	S	E		T	E	E	N	A	G	E
T	O	O	N	I	E		S	T	A	N	D	B	A	G
E	N	D	E	A	R		H	I	R	E		R	I	G
N	I	P			B	A	R	S		L	E	N	S	
S	E	E	D		B	O	R	E		W	A	R	S	
E	D	G	E		O	N	E		S	E	T	A	T	
		M	A	D	E		M	I	C	E				
	P	H	O	N	Y		B	I	L		S	C	R	G
	R	E	E	D		S	I	N	K		T	O	O	L
T	E	E	D		B	C	G	I		N	B	A		
D	F	L		L	O	R	E		B	I	T	T	E	R
R	E	T	A	I	N	E	D		A	D	H	E	R	E
P	R	O	T	E	G	E		T	O	A	S	T		
	S	E	A	S	O	N		S	L	I	T			

PUZZLE 20

T	W	A	Y		F	L	A	T		W	E	A	R
A	G	R	O		F	L	E	S	H		I	A	G	A
P	A	I	D		R	A	I	S	E		S	G	E	G
S	I	D	E	B	E	T		O	B	S	C	E	N	E
			L	O	S	T		R	E	P	O	R	T	
A	G	D		C	E	R	T	A	I	N				
G	O	O	D		A	N	Y		R	E	S	I	S	T
E	N	T	E	R		D			L	I	N	E	R	
S	E	E	S	A	W		E	L	S		N	N	G	A
		I	N	A	P	R	I	L		S	A	Y		
M	A	G	G	I	E		M	I	S	S				
B	E	N	N	E	T	T		I	C	I	N	E	S	S
E	D	G	A		I	R	A	T	E		A	R	E	A
D	I	E	T		N	O	T	E	D		P	I	N	G
S	A	L	E		G	L	A	D		S	E	T	S	

PUZZLE 21

```
ADDS  SWAT   EAGLE
GOOP  LICE   ALLAN
EMERGENCE    SPORT
DESIRED  CHI   AGE
    NAVY  HOLSTER
MAGGIE  SORYU
GROIN  AMID   BDDG
MEAN  PLACE   SOIL
TALE  LORE   STONE
    SLANT  CHARGE
TEASING   SHIN
OLD  TSW  HURTREP
AIMAT  IDENTICAL
STILL  TREK   AGRO
TENSE  HIPS   LAST
```

PUZZLE 22

```
LOTS   SCUM   BITS
IDOL  CHINA   OMIT
ROPE  LEARN   NAGA
ARSENAL  INTEGER
    POST  PEEPER
CAP   SEVERAL
HULK  CRO  SMAILS
IRONS   L   STAIN
PAYOLA  VET   EGAD
    WILSONS   ARG
  CANDLE  THUD
CONNECT  RIPENED
OVGA  ATPAR   BORE
TERM  PLANT   TGTS
STYE  SENT    SASK
```

PUZZLE 23

```
SPED  BHGC   CHASE
HAVE  EARL   HEFTY
ANAL  LURE   ARGUE
MEDICAL  ARMBAND
ELEVATE   ROB
    EVER  STELLAR
  CARED   ARNOLD
ALE         NOV
MARTIN    STAGE
TWOACES   CHAT
    IAN  LIKABLE
ATLANTA  ONEIRON
BEIGE  CGSI   LAST
BASES  KEEN   OVER
AMASS  SNDG   RORY
```

PUZZLE 24

```
    CAD      NQV
TARGET  JUDA   GT
DESIRE   MILLER
INSTORE  GENUINE
SNOT  TIER   ASIA
HIRED  ANTI  TAUT
  STRUT  SUCCESS
    SHOTPAR
  BATTERY  LOWER
RIGA  FALL   COVET
OVEN  ITEM   ROLE
PENLINE  JACKLIN
ENTIRE   WAIVED
DS  NOSY   BARNES
    ENT     YRG
```

PUZZLE 25

```
F E S S   M I S T   A L F
C O U N T   A N T E   W I G C
A R R A Y   S T A R   T E L L
S M O K E   T R U M P   A   A
T A P E   N E O N   L I N K S
T E S T E R   C H A R G E S
    H A S   H E C K L E D
  F A C E T   R I S E N
T O T A L E D   B O N
O U T L I N E   L E G E N D
P R O M O   E T A S   L E E R
O   R   N I P I T   A G A M E
F A N G   P A T H   S A L O N
F L E E   O G L E   S T O N E
  A Y E   D E E R   T O N S
```

PUZZLE 26

```
C C D G     I     A M F G
A L O E   B I G S   S O U R
L E A P   L A M P   S O R E
L A S T M A N   O P E N I N G
A R T H U R   R O O T   O A R
N U T   S E V E N S   J U D O
  P O S E   L E S S U S E D
D   O U T S I D E I N   Y
E S T I M A T E   P E C K
M E A L   G I V E U P   H I T
O A K   H O P E   S E C E D E
S T E P O N E   S I D E A R M
T O M S   N O O N   A T O P
L U G E   D U N G   S E C T
E T A S   T     P E R K
```

PUZZLE 27

```
S M G D   J A G A   A S G C A
D O O R   H E R B   S T R A P
T R E E   T R U E   T R A S H
V E R S A   A N D W R I S T
    S C O T T   H O P P E R
S P L U R G E   L I K E
L O O P E R S   P R E S S E D
U S A         E T A
G E N E S I S   T H E B E A R
  D O N S   A G A I N S T
D E P I C T   G N A R L
  R A T I O N A L   S L O W S
M O V I E   S T I R   I G S T
I D I O T   G O N G   O L G A
D E N N Y   A R E A   N E A R
```

PUZZLE 28

```
A D O R E   T O G O   A S G A
P I L E D   W W G C   P G A C
C R O C S   O N C E   P A W N
D E F I N E   E S A S T A K E
      T E N G R A N D
T H R E E D O   G E A R S
G E O   D E E T S   C A B I N
C A B S   D R O P S   T O N E
S P O I L   S E A T S   U S A
A S T R O   T A I N T E D
      G A P W E D G E
M E D I O C R E   S N A C K S
G R O G   T I D A   A T O N E
T I E S   O D G C   L E V E E
T E S T   R E E K   S N E E D
```

PUZZLE 29

	D	E	R	K			A	C	C	E	S	S
	L	E	V	E	E		T	A	I	N	T	E	D
D	E	F	I	N	E		C	A	R	T	G	A	T	E
W	A	L	L	O	P		A	N	D	Y		T	T	F
A	G	A			L	T	D	S			J	U	L	Y
R	U	T	S		D	U	E	T		S	O	R	E
F	E	E	T		E	R	R		C	A	K	E	D
		A	G	E	E		S	O	M	E
	S	T	R	U	T		M	I	N		R	U	B	S
	P	O	R	T		B	I	T	E		S	P	U	N
G	O	R	Y		P	A	L	E			A	R	E
R	I	P		H	I	R	E		S	P	O	N	G	E
E	L	E	M	E	N	T	S		L	A	N	D	E	D
M	E	D	I	A	T	E			O	C	C	U	R
	D	O	C	T	O	R			B	E	E	P

PUZZLE 30

A	R	M	S			A	P	C	D		D	A	S	H
D	O	U	P		S	T	E	E	R		I	G	P	A
D	O	T	E		M	A	G	N	A		G	A	I	N
S	T	E	N	S	O	N		S	I	G	N	I	N	G
			T	A	K	E		O	N	L	I	N	E
W	B	H		E	N	T	R	E	A	T
G	O	O	F		D	D	E		D	R	A	W	A	L
T	A	P	A	S			P		E	R	O	D	E
F	R	E	S	C	A		E	P	A		Y	O	G	A
	H	A	T	H	E	A	D			D	O	D
	F	A	I	L	T	O		N	D	G	A
R	O	B	O	P	R	O		T	O	P	D	E	C	K
I	R	O	N		A	P	R	O	N		A	B	L	E
S	A	V	E		C	L	O	N	E		P	A	I	N
E	Y	E	D		T	A	M	E			T	Y	P	O

PUZZLE 31

A	N	T	I		D	R	I	P		C	A	B	L	E
J	O	I	N		R	I	G	A		A	D	L	I	B
A	P	P	R	A	I	S	A	L		P	L	A	N	E
R	E	S	E	R	V	E		M	A	P		M	E	R
		A	M	E	N		T	H	E	B	E	S	T
W	O	N	D	E	R		T	R	A	D	E
A	V	O	I	D		C	O	E	N		N	A	G	A
T	E	N	N		S	O	W	E	D		C	L	O	D
T	R	E	E		T	O	E	S		B	R	O	A	D
		S	T	A	L	L		S	L	E	E	T	Y
P	A	S	S	A	G	E		S	T	U	N
A	D	P		W	E	R		P	R	E	S	S	E	D
C	O	U	L	D		B	L	U	E	S	H	A	D	E
E	R	R	O	R		A	U	R	A		A	F	G	A
D	E	N	N	Y		G	G	T	M		W	E	A	R

PUZZLE 32

L	E	G	S			C	A	K	E		H	A	G	S
E	A	R	N		P	A	P	E	R		A	G	R	O
S	G	A	A		O	T	H	E	R		P	A	I	N
S	T	A	R	T	L	E		G	A	S	P	I	N	G
		L	A	I	R		A	T	T	E	N	D
A	L	P		T	E	R	N	I	O	N
R	I	O	T		E	D	U		C	L	I	E	N	T
C	R	O	W	S			S			E	N	T	E	R
H	A	R	O	L	D		S	C	S		G	A	G	A
	P	E	E	K	O	U	T			S	A	P
	S	L	E	E	V	E		S	A	G	S
S	H	A	R	K	I	E		T	I	G	H	T	E	N
P	A	R	S		A	P	R	O	N		O	O	Z	E
A	R	G	O		T	E	A	M	S		T	R	G	A
T	E	E	N		E	R	T	S			S	N	O	T

PUZZLE 33

```
B R A G   D S G A   S W I F T
R U L E   E L E C   E A G L E
A N O N   L I A R   R I S E N
K I N E T I C   O M I T T E D
E N G R A V E   S E O
      A C E D   S T U T T E R
  C O L O R     A S S U M E
B A G             R I P
C A R I N G     S L A N T
O N E W O O D   S L I T
      C O O   P A N A C H E
B A G H A N G   O N E I R O N
A C T O R   L E N D   L A S T
S M A R T   E D G E   O V E R
S E A N S   G O E R   R E L Y
```

PUZZLE 34

```
    R O M       D R S
  S T A D I A   B E A T   D F
H A R M O N       S C O R E R
I N A P R I L   I T E R A T E
N D G A     B C G I   A G E S
T R I N E   T O O T   G O S H
A C T A S   S T U D E N T
      R E S T A T E
  S P I N A C H   E N D O F
S T I R   T O E D   T E P I D
M O V E   B U R N   V E T O
A R O L L E R   A G A I N S T
R E T A I L     O O S T I E
T D   N E T S   T A K E O N
    D D S       S I R
```

PUZZLE 35

```
  P A P A   T E N T   A M A
C I G A R   A Q U A   H E R D
A L E R T   L U M P   A N T E
R E N O S   L I B E L   W   C
B U D D   R I P E   A D O R E
  P A Y F E E   R E G I M E N
    O D D   S U G G E S T
  S H O R E     G I A N T
C H E A T E R   D E N
A I R T I M E   A N G L E S
R A I S E   L I N E   O N T O
I   T   S T I M P   H O G A N
N C A A   R E A L   U N I T E
G O G I   O V G A   N I N E S
  G E R   T E E N   T E E S
```

PUZZLE 36

```
  A F G A     W     A C R E
C Z A R   A G E S   C O E N
L A N E   S E M I   A W G C
A L B E R T A   M I S S I L E
S E A T E R   B I T E   M O N
H A S   N O H O L E   R E S T
  S E A T   D A M P E N E R
S   P E T T E R S E N     Y
T R A P D O O R   L O A F
R E N T   T R E N C H   T I P
A M Y   H A R K   H A V A N A
P O T H O L E   S E M I N A R
  D I S S   N S G A   D E N T
  E M I T   T A U T   E N C Y
  L E G S     T   M O D E
```

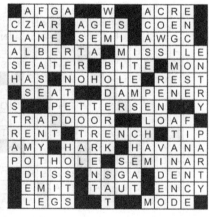

PUZZLE 37

```
H A N D . I G S T . S P A C E
A G E E . S I L O . A R R O W
L E A F . S L E W . V E N U E
E S T E S . F E N C E D I N .
. N O T O K . S P I E T H . .
P L A S T E R . P G A C . . .
M O R E A N D . C A R T F E E
G A M . . . . . . . . L A Y .
A N Y C L U B . F A N B A S E
. H O S S . E M E R G E D . .
V A C A T E . T R Y T O . . .
. P O R T R A I T . S T A S H
I R A T E . R E I D . H I D E
L O S E R . M U L E . E D G A
E N T R Y . S P E C . R E A D
```

PUZZLE 38

```
B L A R E . W C M A . P U R E
J A D E D . B L E D . A N A L
A M A S S . H E R O . P I C K
D E M O N S . A I R W A V E S
. . R E P O R T E D . . . . .
A M A T E U R . . G O O D S .
L A G . D R I L L . C O B R A
O N E S . N O T E S . H A I R
N I N E S . N O T E D . M N G
E A T E N . . G A R B A G E .
. . . D I S H O N O R . . . .
C A R T G A T E . S P I R I T
M I L E . G R A B . P L A N E
D D G A . T I V O . E L I T E
R E A R . O P E N . D O L L S
```

PUZZLE 39

```
. F L I P . . D E P I C T .
. L E A S E . I N A C A R T .
S E R I A L . I N T R E P I D
C A R R O T . D I R T . A G G
A G U . T I N Y . M B G A . .
R U L E . F R O G . S A L E .
F E E L . O U T . D E T E R .
. . T Y R E . B E A T . . . .
. A D O R E . U S A . E R T S
N E R D . G S G F . R E E L .
L I M O . B H G C . C E O . .
A M A . P L O T . A B S E N T
C A R E L E S S . P O L I S H
E L E G A N T . G R A V Y . .
. S T A N D S . M E M E . . .
```

PUZZLE 40

```
B O M B . M A T T . S O R T
A D G A . M O W E R . U N I S
M O W S . A R E N A . B A N K
A R T I C L E . D I S M I S S
. . C O L A . E N T I R E . .
A N D . E N T R E A T . . . .
G R O G . T D A . E S T E E M
S L U R P . B . . H E D G E .
A P P E A L . L T O . D I G A
. A C A S E O F . . T S N . .
A T T E S T . M Y T H . . . .
B L I N D T O . B O B O T I E
L O R E . M O T O R . S D G A
O N E S . A G I L E . T G T S
B E D S . N E X T . S A F E .
```

PUZZLE 41

```
S W A G   A S G A   F I B E R
G A M E   T H I N   E A R L Y
E V E N T T E N T   S N E A D
G E N E R A L   E T C   A T E
      R A I L   L A U N D E R
S T R A I N   P O L E E
D R I L L   P O P E   R E D S
G G G T   C O R E S   V E E P
C A S E   E L K S   P O K E R
      R E L A Y   C R U S T Y
S L A M M E R   G O O S
L O S   B B B   R U N N I N G
U N T I L   E M E R G E N C E
M E R G E   A G E S   S F G A
P R O A M   R U D E   S O U R
```

PUZZLE 42

```
C L A P   B I T S   O P G A
G O A L   F L A R E   N A I L
C S G A   R U N I N   T R A P
S T A N D I N   F I S H I N G
      S A N D   L O W E S T
G F C   G E N E R A L
A I R S   E R A   S N I T C H
P R I O R   M   S N E A D
E M B L E M   E S P   E A S T
      I N O R D E R   M T V
  A D D O N E   T O S S
T R A N S I T   T P A T O U R
R E N E   T I T L E   E A S E
I N N S   O R D E R   E G G S
P A Y S   R E A D   P A R T
```

PUZZLE 43

```
F L U B   C H U B   D O M E D
R O S E   A O K I   E V A D E
A G I F   R L G A   V E R G E
M I N I M A L   S T I N K E R
E N G R A V E   E R A
      S T A R   S A T I S F Y
  E A T E N   P E R B A G
M A R         G M T
F R I S C O   P O S S E
O L D S A L T   S E A T
      T G A   P A T R O N S
C H A P E A U   I N H I B I T
S A V O R   G G F U   P A P A
G R I P E   H E F T   E M I T
A D D E D   T O Y S   D A T E
```

PUZZLE 44

```
    L D A       W E B
  C H O I C E   H E A R   B O
C L E V E R       E R A S E R
A E R A T E S   P I N C H E D
B A R B   P G A C   K A N E
S T O L E   H O N E   E V E R
  S N E A K   L I M I T E R
      G O L F C A P
  C A T T R A P   N O L I E
P U R R   N C A A   D E N N Y
E R I E   F E L L   A P G A
P L E A S E D   T E R R A I N
P E S T E R     D I N I N G
Y D   E A R L   E U G E N E
    D R Y       C A D
```

PUZZLE 45

C	H	I	P		D	G	C	R		E	W	E	
S	H	O	N	E		E	R	I	E		M	E	N	A
T	I	T	L	E		S	I	T	E		S	B	G	S
I	N	A	I	R		S	P	I	L	L		S		P
R	U	I	N		J	E	E	Z		A	G	I	L	E
	P	R	E	F	E	R		E	R	R	A	T	I	C
		L	E	T		N	E	G	L	E	C	T	
	S	T	E	A	L			G	E	E	S	E	
A	E	R	A	T	E	S		C	R	S			
S	T	A	R	L	E	T		L	I	T	T	L	E
C	H	I	L	I		A	T	O	P		R	A	S	H
E		L		E	S	T	E	S		L	O	T	T	A
N	A	I	L		P	U	R	E		O	U	T	E	R
D	I	N	O		A	R	M	S		S	P	E	E	D
	D	G	U		T	E	S	T		T	E	R	M	

PUZZLE 46

S	M	O	G		R		A	B	A	D	
S	C	A	N		S	L	O	P		L	O	R	E
T	O	E	S		C	O	C	A		L	O	T	S
A	R	S	E	N	A	L		T	H	E	T	I	P	S
L	E	T	T	E	R		G	R	I	N		C	I	T
E	R	R		W	E	A	R	O	N		A	L	S	O
	S	O	B	S		E	N	G	I	N	E	E	R
U		R	E	P	R	E	S	E	N	T			M
N	I	N	E	T	E	E	N		P	E	S	T	
C	R	O	W		S	P	I	R	A	L		C	R	S
L	O	S		M	O	R	E		C	A	S	H	I	T
E	N	C	L	O	S	E		D	A	Y	T	O	N	A
	M	O	A	T		S	B	G	S		O	L	I	D
	A	R	G	O		S	I	T	E		R	A	T	S
	N	E	A	R		B			V	E	R	Y	

PUZZLE 47

D	G	P	I		A	B	A	D		S	P	L	A	T
I	R	O	N		T	U	N	E		T	R	I	B	E
G	A	L	S		L	I	N	E		R	U	N	I	N
A	D	L	I	B		L	O	P	S	I	D	E	D	
		D	A	D	D	Y		O	P	E	N	E	D	
B	A	R	E	L	I	E		A	M	E	N		
I	N	O	R	D	E	R		R	E	S	T	A	T	E
L	O	L							S	O	D		
E	N	L	A	R	G	E		T	E	N	T	I	N	G
		T	A	L	E		O	P	E	R	A	T	E	
E	S	T	A	T	E		S	P	A	R	E		
	C	O	N	T	E	M	P	T		D	A	R	T	S
P	O	W	E	R		A	R	I	D		T	I	D	E
A	R	E	N	A		T	E	E	D		E	D	G	A
N	E	R	D	Y		H	E	R	S		D	E	A	L

PUZZLE 48

S	I	U	M	P		G	G	C	T		A	L	O	F
M	A	N	O	R		A	U	R	A		N	A	N	A
G	U	I	D	E		L	E	A	P		C	G	C	S
A	T	T	E	S	T		S	T	A	G	E	S	E	T
				S	H	O	R	T	E	S	T		
F	A	S	T	O	N	E			A	M	A	S	S
E	G	U		T	I	N	G	E		A	R	G	U	E
A	R	I	D		C	O	U	L	D		S	I	G	A
S	E	T	A	T		S	T	I	R	S		L	G	N
T	E	E	N	Y			H	E	I	R	E	S	S
		P	E	R	S	U	A	D	E			
M	E	S	M	E	R	I	C		D	E	P	A	R	T
A	R	E	A		A	L	E	C		A	L	F	I	E
D	I	E	S		S	E	N	D		R	A	G	O	N
E	E	K	S		E	Y	E	S		M	Y	A	T	T

PUZZLE 49

PUZZLE 50

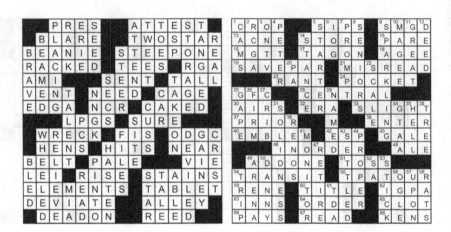

DESIGNER INK – ALL AGES BOOKS
HOMESCHOOL INK – SCHOOL BOOKS
SUPER KIDZ – KIDS BOOKS

designerinkbooks@gmail.com

Quotes   Theme

| Books | "Designer Ink" sports | |

Search AMAZON today! or

Type into Amazon

Amazon Standard ID Number

B08L3XCCMC   **Nov 2021**   **B08P15YF7K**   **B086PTBBBW**

B089TTYR34   **B089M5Z58C**   **B085K78C6Y**   **B08PJK7CWM**

ALL SPORTS
MOVIES
CAMPING – HIKING
FISHING – HUNTING
USA   CANADA
CATS – PETS
ALL HOLIDAYS

CROSSWORD
WORD SEARCH
SUDOKU
LARGE PRINT
KIDS WS
KIDS MAZES
KIDS COLORING

FB: @DESIGNERINKBOOKS

Made in the USA
Monee, IL
12 December 2024

73497388R00066